13:3

Joshua Underwood

WESTBOW
PRESS®
A DIVISION OF THOMAS NELSON
& ZONDERVAN

WestBow Press books may be ordered through booksellers or by contacting:

WestBow Press
A Division of Thomas Nelson & Zondervan
1663 Liberty Drive
Bloomington, IN 47403
www.westbowpress.com
844-714-3454

Scripture taken from the King James Version of the Bible.

ISBN: 978-1-6642-3092-7 (sc)
ISBN: 978-1-6642-3094-1 (hc)
ISBN: 978-1-6642-3093-4 (e)

Library of Congress Control Number: 2021907600

Print information available on the last page.

WestBow Press rev. date: 06/21/2021

Foreword

In 2016, while pastoring in an inner-city community, I met Joshua Underwood. I immediately saw that God's hand was all over his life. A life marked with deep adversity, struggle and challenges yet rooted in the author and perfecter of his faith, Christ. After facing life plus 145 years and ultimately receiving a 15-year prison sentence, Joshua came out of prison with a zeal and a passion to glorify God.

After countless prison stories, I began to realize that the men behind bars were just as Godly and Christ-like as the ones interwoven in everyday society. In September 2018, I had the opportunity to go minister in Desoto Correctional Institution for the first time ever. I walked out realizing that the men behind bars ministered to me more than I could ever minister to them and that the most genuine Christian community I have ever experienced was inside the cell block. Acts 4:34 became so real. "And there was no needy among them." I saw the young giving up their chairs for the old, the old encouraging the young to find their hope in Christ and in Christ alone. I saw a band of brothers willing to give up their life for one another and for the sake of the gospel. I saw true joy amidst people serving life sentences. I saw gratitude in those that got the opportunity to serve in the chaplain. The very same things we take for granted was life to their souls.

We live in a society today, where we are marked and defined by our mistakes. We tend to label people by their failures and shortcomings. Those labels are astronomically heightened when referring to prisoners.

We label them by their conviction: murderers, thieves, felons, convicts, etc. We tend to think that people can't change or won't change but we never dive one step into their story, to understand why, to hear their pain and struggle. We write them off thinking: "they're paying for what they did" yet we forget that we (those outside of prison) sit blameless before God because of Christ, just as they do. That we, ultimately don't pay the consequences for our own shortcomings and sins but that it's covered by the blood of the Lamb.

This book is a call to remember those behind chains. To remember that no one is too far gone from the reach of Christ. That even a murderer does not have to be remembered as a murderer or even labeled that way, but they can be seen like the apostle Paul, who isn't remembered by an act of murder rather an ambassador for Christ. Behind those bars are men and woman who have been transformed by the power of the gospel. In this book you will see 15 years of stories, poems, spoken words, artists, composers and talented individuals that will be remembered by their prison ID rather than their God given talent.

I pray that this book spurs something deep in your soul and moves you to action, to care and love those behind bars, to remove any label and stigma we place on prisoners. "Remember those in prison, as if you were together with them in prison..." – Hebrews 13:3a

Jared Rendon

Intro

This is my journey... my fears, my dreams, my hopes, my prayers, my pain, my joy, my flaws, my weaknesses, my strengths... Face at best & Face at worst... One thing is certain. Upon my honor, everything captured on these pages will be the truth, the whole truth and nothing but the truth, so help me God... So whatever you read in the Face Book can be taken at Face Value...

Who is Face? Well, as any real artist would do, rather than define myself, I will paint you pictures, tell you stories, and convey intimate thoughts... In doing so, I'll allow you to reach your own conclusions and form your own opinions... There will undoubtedly be twists and turns, up and downs, highs and lows...

Featured artists... This is life from my vantage point, the world through my eyes... at times, you'll see the poet, at times you'll see a man of strength struggling to overcome weakness... You'll see a man of tremendous faith battling crippling doubt... Perhaps, you'll be deeply moved at times, inspired at others, taken aback... That's the beauty of this journey... We have no specific destination... No particular route to follow, no script to adhere to ... Why? Because life isn't about the destination, but the journey... Every experience, every emotion, every detour, every moment has significance... Glean what you can from my journey and the journey of whoever else happens to venture onto these pages... Maybe your story and mine are similar... Maybe you relate when you hear me speak of love, and God, and pain, and prison...

Maybe you've been in chains... Maybe you have your own prison that doesn't consist of razor-wire fences... Maybe as I convey my methods for coping, and the hope that has enabled me to stand tall and remain solid, it will speak to you in a way that inspires, encourages, and enlightens you to overcome your battle, whether our stories are the same or not... Maybe your story is more moving and inspiring than mine, and you're capable of telling it better... My prayer, then, is that you become the artist and I become your audience, that my story could be enriched... For now, buckle up...

Imagine a Place

Imagine a place where the sun never sets, and the sun never rises... Where the moon is eclipsed, and the stars never shine... A foreign land, where rainbows do not wash away the rain. Can you think of a place where every day is the same..? Picture Christmas with no gifts, Thanksgiving with no dish, Valentine's with no kiss, and birthdays with no wish... An insipid world, where adults act like kids... And kids aren't given the opportunity to enjoy their adolescence and live... This world gives no breaks, and has no brakes when it spins – it moves unbelievably fast... Passes you by and leaves you stuck in the past... Its future looks hopeless, because in this place, hopelessness spreads like a rash... Visualize this place where friends become strangers, and a wrong look invites danger... An unfruitful land, where all fruits are bitter, and even food has no flavor... Where ignorance is contagious and because of it, violence does not faze you... But what will it be, "You"? *Faith* or *Fate*? One of them must save you... But start with the mirror, where your reflection can change you... Yet, the mirrors in this strange place are all stained, filthy and cracked – so they reflect hurtful facts... Nevertheless, you are faced with two options – you act, or react... This place will mislead you – please keep your priorities in-tact... In this world, your perception will blur... In here, there are no secrets – every word is heard... Now, this might sound absurd, but I have seen you here before... All the prolific specifics of your characteristics have walked through those doors... This world does it exist – its realistically explicit... You just never noticed because yours is materialistic... Don't be a hero to your ego and become another statistic... Let me be your witness in this world that is wicked... But first, lose yourself, find your spirit, and learn to let your soul listen...

"Echo"

Dear Journal

As I hold you in my hands and spend time with you, I'm touched by the thoughts and feelings you have provoked from others. I marvel, really, because many of the thoughts have been my own thoughts; many of these feelings, I have felt. I'm feeling you.

You are amazing! You are a light in this cold, dark place. You are drink to the thirsty, rest to the weary, salve to the hurting. You are a mirror wherein I behold myself in the thoughts and experiences and feelings of others. How do you do that?!

You are like the spring flower that freely offers of its sweet nectar, knowing full that the thirsty will drink, will be refreshed, and will ultimately and unknowingly, be your servant and will carry your burden, and will feed others. You are a delight, and I thank you. You are deep. You speak of pain and love and fear and God in a way that I can relate. You speak of the senselessness of this place, this sentence, and this life that is no life at all. And in your speaking, you are my friend. You share my interest. You voice my ideas in the words of others. You, in these pages exemplify that friendship of a superior mind that exalts the lower character, enlarges the horizon of thought, and makes life worthy, more active, more interesting. I need this.

You are a reminder that, though physically captive, our minds are free to soar the heights and to sound the depths. You are a reminder that, even here, in this sad and humiliating place, we may think and love and suffer and live inwardly, deeply.

You are a call to awaken, to rise up, to think, and to live. I have heard your call, and now hope to spend more time with you. Thank you for finding me.

W.R.

Prison is Like War

Like an involuntary draft, none of us choose to be here... Granted, with exception of those who are innocent of their alleged crimes (& there ARE countless innocent men doing time for crimes they did not commit), most of us were brought here as a direct result of our actions. However, the fact remains, we were brought here, and are kept here, against our will - like prisoners of war...

Like soldiers in the military, we live in an environment that is hostile, adversarial, and routine. Hostile, because we are subjected to obey authority figures who believe it is their sole purpose - and seemingly make it their aim in life - to oppress, degrade, dehumanize, and carry out punishment upon those in their charge. Adversarial, because those who are subjected to the degradation and oppression are HUMANS, who feel, and who have dreams, and desires, and needs... Men who were abandoned by their family, forsaken by their friends... Men who find themselves at the mercy of those who continuously abuse their discretion. Men whose flames of hope continue to dwindle and flicker, in eyes that used to be ablaze with promise and potential. Men who sit on the sidelines of life, as seasons vanish, and hope is placed on life support. Years of disappointment, frustrated expectations, suppressed desires, severed relationships, shattered dreams, lost loved ones... And men become hardened, calloused... Angry... Their perspective begins to be molded, jaded, indurated... When a man is continuously subjected to such circumstances, he begins to view almost everyone as an adversary. When this man is placed in-the-midst of 1,500 other men with similar stories and struggles... The entire atmosphere becomes adversarial...

There are casualties here. Men die; usually violently, always alone. Almost always senselessly and in vain... I've watched a few soldiers fall behind these lines... Nica, Fyah, Earl... Countless others, who - to the outside world - are just nameless, faceless, pitiful souls.

There is camaraderie here. Brotherhoods can be found. Even in-the-midst of these suffering souls, compassion can be found. Loyalty exists. Good deeds take place. Occasionally, soldiers' paths cross, their stories intersect, battles are fought, rations are shared... In these rare times, men whose hearts were almost completely dark from pain and loss and disillusionment are reminded of good... brotherhoods are formed... Men suffer, fight battles and break bread together, and become brothers in the struggle...

My emergence is approaching. My tour in this battlefield is almost up... But my experiences have left indelible marks on my life. Eleven and a half years!!! One and a half to go.

But I have formed those bonds. I have shared those struggles. I've learned the names and stories of society's nameless. I've met men of incredible intellect, plentiful potential, phenomenal faith... I've watched good soldiers die bad deaths...

Like a soldier whose comrades died behind enemy lines, while he was fortunate enough to escape with his own life... There is a sort of Survivor's Guilt. A certain knowledge that I don't deserve a second chance, any more than my comrades - who will never get one. There is a realization that my opportunity is not a result of my character, skill, or talent- but God's grace alone.

With that knowledge comes a sense of burden... A fire burning within, that compels me to accomplish what my comrades can't, so they can live vicariously through Face. My comrades need pictures for their albums, soups for that late-night stomach rumbling, pen pals for companionship, funds for lawyer fees...

"Remember Those Who Are in Chains, As
Though You Were in Chains with Them"
Hebrews 13:3

Write!

"Write! Write!!" A voice keeps telling me *write...* Compelling me to *write,* to tell em about my plight... Even when my eyes are heavy late at night, I must *write...* In case I never reach the mic- incase I never reach the prize, even though I paid the price... *"Write, write!!"* Just let my mind take flight, late night, poor light... The precise reason why I possess poor sight... Because I *write...* Because my future isn't promised, even though it looks bright... Because my hands are tied, my feet are chained, and my pen is my only weapon in this fight... Because I'm the middle man in a position to reach both Black and White... *"Write, write!!"* Because my peers are teaching them wrong, somebody gotta tell em right... Rappers give you death for free, but pastors recording the Gospel & selling life... *"Write!"* Until my hand cramps, my eyes burn, and my neck is tight... In an effort that I might reach a new height... *I "write"* that souls may be stirred and revival might ignite... That my audience might allow the Bible to get down inside em and enlight... Providing insight, guidance and survival in this life. I *"write!"* because I know what its like... Because I been there and I know if they keep striving, everything will be alright... I *"write!"* for the child frightened by the sirens and the lights... For the young girl tryna fight off her father, who is tryna slide up inside her at night... *"Write, write!"* Mothers are crying over their young ones dying in gun fights... Fathers doing time, serving life, wearing stripes... The harvest is white & the timing is ripe... So *"Write!"*

Earl

Today wasn't the best of days... My friend, Earl, who has been down 24 years, jumped on an officer. He's been discouraged lately, and I should have seen the signs that he was nearing his breaking point... He has been doing all he can to get back in court... But his lawyer died 2 months ago, and his family isn't helping as they should. He's been quiet, stand off-ish lately. He buckled under the pressure...

I can't help but wonder if I was too caught up in my own issues, too focused, on my problems, my comfort, my freedom... To be of any use to someone like Earl, with very little hope, and no promise of a future on Earth... And he is a professed Christian... It's a sad day when believers (myself included) are too wrapped up in their own affairs to notice the desperate pleas for help, the signs of despair in those around us... Lord, forgive me.

"Think Outside of The Box"

Society is constantly boxing us in ... Categorizing, criticizing, discriminating, underestimating, stereotyping... Labeling us as POOR, or UNEDUCATED, or as a CONVICTED FELON... Or, because you grew up without a father, or in a dysfunctional family, or for various other reasons...

They reduce us (When I say 'us', I am referring to those who've been stereotyped... And when I say "Them", I am referring to those who do the stereotyping.) When they reduce us to numbers... To statistics... When they make deductions about us based on our perceived social, financial, racial, religious, or any other status - they 'Box Us In...'

Oftentimes, those "BOXES" or various forms of oppression result in physical boxes... Juvenile detention centers... Boot camps... Prison... They "Box Us In" ... And, sadly, after time, those boxes begin to have a profound effect on one's thinking. Men spend so much time in a "box" that they've lost the ability to think outside the box... So deep in the box, they have no hope of getting out. (A man w/ no hope is among the most dangerous men - but that is another story altogether)

We eventually reach that stage because there are only two options - or, rather 2 types of mentalities in prison... Though, there are countless mentalities, personalities, idiosyncrasies, various levels of mental illness and psychosis... So, perhaps its better still, if we say; every man in a social box (specifically, prison) falls into 2 broad categories.

Category #1 Those Tryna Get OUT of Prison:

My bad, lemme mention the other category 1st...

Those Tryna Get Comfortable IN the Box

Before I go any further, allow me to dive deeper, as to the cause of these boxes...

Prison lifestyle cultivates the behavior patterns, and conditions the mind to THINK INSIDE THE BOX... They do this through various rules... Rules that are designed to suppress individuality, prohibit unity, forbid independence, etc... They create an environment that is demoralizing, degrading... and it affects the psyche... Minds begin to adapt... To "adapt" can be a blessing or a curse... More accurately, a God- given ability- a blessing - that we've allowed the enemy to use against us...

They place things in our box that help us adapt... To name a few: TV, board games, telephones, MP3s, jewelry, sports, religion... and we begin to adapt, and to wrap our minds around all these things IN THE BOX... Our attention is diverted, we become distracted, and grow past "adapting", to becoming comfortable and complacent, and focusing our time and resources on the things that are IN THE BOX... On obtaining these things IN THE BOX, to increasing our level of comfort IN THE BOX... and we've begun to THINK INSIDE THE BOX...

Then, there are those who focus on GETTING OUT OF THE BOX...

To name a few: those who study law... Read... Further their education... Pursue vocations... Focus on personal development... those who truly seek, find, worship, and serve God... Those who maintain roles (however minimal) that transcend razor-wire fences... Roles like husband, father, rapper, plumber, teacher, etc. All of those whose time and resources are spent in not only maintaining these roles IN THE BOX, but on

GETTING OUT OF THE BOX... Essentially, those who THINK OUTSIDE THE BOX.

It's the same in society, people are trapped in boxes; poor people, disabled people, convicted people. We're placed in boxes because we're a minority, or because we're a "statistic..." And the boxes we're placed in, the stereotypes society gives us affect our thinking... We begin thinking within the social, economic, or professional, or educational parameters set by society. If we're hood, we strive only for those things obtainable and accessible in the hood, generally speaking... If you're in the hood, your ambitions normally revolve around your BOX... We rob, and we sell dope, and club, and put rims on cars, buy jewelry, make it rain, and spend tens of thousands on wardrobes... If you got $50,000, a car worth that, and an apartment where you pay rent, you eating- you're good...

People outside OUR BOX own private jets, mansions, corporations, restaurants, the apartments we pay rent in... People who are millionaires and billionaires... People who are not defined or limited by society's boxes... People who THINK OUTSIDE THE **BOX...**

Proverbs says, "as a man thinketh, so is he". Thoughts become actions, become behaviors, become habits, become lifestyles... So, it begins with THINKING OUTSIDE THE BOX...

We GOTTA break the cycles, We GOTTA expose ourselves and our children to things outside of our box... We GOTTA live lives transcendent of our beginnings... we GOTTA teach our children to strive to reach for the stars, to pursue their dreams, to believe in themselves and THINK OUTSIDE THE BOX... FEEL ME?

Earl Pt. 2

Earl is dead. Period. Earl is gone... He assaulted an officer 3 weeks ago, was taken to Florida State Prison... And is now dead. No one knows the particulars of what happened, nor are we likely to ever know... The officials say it was suicide. Everyone who knows Earl rejects that explanation vehemently. Except me... I mean, I am not eagerly accepting the official report, and calling it truth... I've been in this system for eleven years. I know the consequences of attacking "one of them." Their motto is, "We Never Walk Alone". Earl hurt one of them; now he is dead...

On the other hand, he was suffering from severe depression... He has been giving up hope... The day he jumped on the C/0 was the day he waived the white flag on life. Its over. A good, solid, humble, soft spoken, God-fearing man, who became just another victim of the system... Just another morsel in the Belly of The Beast

5/21/13

Ced's Story

Unfortunately, I wasn't born with a silver spoon... Yet, I'm thankful for every obstacle, every bit of pain, the joy, as well as this very day that I'm blessed with... So many paths I've taken - so many attributes awaken... But, what I truly seek is the love of the Most High before I'm taken... Its knowledge of self that allows me to acknowledge the fact that we humans are perfectly imperfect... But, I personally refuse to use such an excuse - I just keep working... Towards a better life, a better me... Striving to obtain the mental and physical tools necessary to become victorious in the quest which will set me free... This battle is one I was destined to fight: Its me versus me... You see, the old me has been my downfall, my enemy... And if I allow him to win, he will certainly be the death of me... May I explain? That he cannot be the sole recipient, for I too am to blame... For the numerous acts from my past that I cannot change... I go King James... After missing a shot in the last seconds, I dissect it and correct it for the next game...

Yet, my life isn't as simple as a ball-game... For my acts, I received the max and now I reside in the "chain-gang"... The judge told me life-was it just? Was it right? But alright, I won't complain... I have no choice but to charge-it-to-the-game... Yes, the same game that claimed to love me and only me... Then, turned on me - stabbed me in the back when things got ugly... But somehow I was able to pick up the pieces that were left, and I found myself... Finally, I stand, a true man, with plans to make the best of the hand I was dealt... I've seen the bottom of the bottom; all that's left is to strive for the top of the top... As I climb, I rewind in my mind, and say a prayer for those for whom the clock has completely stopped... Victims of ignorance, victims of self, victims of the block... Which shall never bear your name... I hate to be the bearer of bad news; but that chapter was in vain... I must keep myself free from those very chains... They threaten to choke me, cutting off the very oxygen I need for my brain... I hope to fly better yet soar, and to do so, I need wings... Not like those of a bird, but a means of overcoming adversity - the ability to truly think... Its been a long time coming and I'm quite thankful for all the events of my life as well the lesson I've been given... At this time, I feel you're familiar with my friend and brother Face, allow me to introduce you to Yadi: Better known as...

-Cedrick Scrivens

Sinner's Prayer

Lawd, it's been a rough couple... Days filled with thangs that made me wish I had a stunt double... And made me say, "Lawd, haven't I been through enough trouble??? And enough struggle to cry a river of tears, for a month of Sundays?" Another summer where tempers flare like the temperature... So, mean mugs, heated glances, and cold glares here are plentiful... And the recipients, that receive those glares are usually immature... Or, at best possess communication skills that are minimal... Who grow frustrated cause their continual... Efforts to express themselves normal, fizzle into the physical... Combine that with differences, from race to religion, and altercations become rituals... Really, tho... Lawd, may I have a word with you?... In the quiet, all alone, hop in the two-seater, and just swerve with You... I could really use a word from you... I admit I been driving a little careless, swerving, ran over a curb or two ... Blew up at my woman, said some unseemly things, I know you heard me, too... That's why I'm here, dedicating this spoken word to You... There is no other Word but You... Nobody spoke and created the Earth, but You... Nobody spoke light into darkness, and life into dirt... but You... So I'm here, at the throne, your feet with no pretense... To repent and put a cease to this sequence of events... That have simultaneously been causing You grief, and leaving me spent... In need of strength, forgiveness & restoration... and You hear me, and You feel me, and You grant my request with no hesitation... Not because You're some genie in a bottle, who blesses according to how we feel... But, 'cause You made me, You molded me, You know my heart, and it's real... You got me, and you hold me down, and I'm thankful that You're there... Cause You're so good, and I'm so glad that You hear a sinner's prayer...

Belly of the Beast

Resting in the bowels of this over-stuffed leviathan... Where, from the meekest to the vilest men, society continues to pile us in... Surrounded by crime and sin... Fallen, praying for the day when I can rise again... like Lazarus, coming forth from the same cave I've watched others dying in... Lord, you are my Rock of Gibraltar... My Foundation when I slip and my balance is altered... Your spirit keeps me, even when my flesh falters... When I'm weary form this journey, I find rest upon your altar... ABBA FATHA!!! Comfort me in the midst of my oppression... Deliver me from this pent-up aggression... Directed at those who make my misery their profession... Meanwhile, use the professors of darkness as instruments to instruct me in your righteous lessons... The woman in my life is regressing... Which is depressing... She says I demand perfection... I say I expect progression... Nevertheless, I guess the blame falls on my mirror's reflection... Hmmm... my minds screaming, "Let her fall and spring into a new season"... but matters of the heart defy logic and love wants nothing to do with reason... So here we are, where we shouldn't be... Futilely fighting to realize what couldn't be... Sometimes, love is pulling the plug before the damage is too great... Once vows are exchanged and rings go on hands, it's too late... Oh well, another bad love gone south... The fat lady's belting another sad love song out...

Oh, Brother, Lord only knows what we're in for... Mother, big brother is peepin' in my window!!! Listenin' to my calls all in my business... Maybe I should put freedom of speech on my wish list... I mean, I ain't tryna start no drama, but why can you disrespect your mama... But can't oppose homosexuality or criticize Obama? Critical times when typical rhymes cross political lines... and faith has no say in politics, but politicians continually cross spiritual lines... Open your eyes!!! See the hope in disguise... Keep your head up, or you'll miss it when he opens the skies...

Mama

I spoke to my mother today... For the second time in 6 years. I haven't seen her in 13 years; embraced her in 14!!! I was 14 then!!! I'm 28 now. She's been in prison, she was addicted to crack cocaine. I spent my childhood watching her smoke crack, sell our food and clothes for crack, prostitute for crack, steal and lie for crack... I've watched her be beaten unconscious, I've seen her raped, I've watched her attempt suicide... I've seen her in handcuffs, visited her behind bars... All as a scared child who was too young to take a stand for her...

Mama's home now (and I'm behind bars, ironically)... But Ol' girl is free, she's been delivered from addiction, she has her own place, and she's married to a man who she says adores her. *God Answers Prayers!!!*

Ma, I know you'll eventually read this. You'll read it for before the world has a chance to. You're my #1 fan... You must've told me a thousand times tonight that you are proud of me. What you don't know, Ma, is that *I'm Your#1 Fan!!* And I am far more proud of you than you'll ever know... I know where we came from. I know what you've been thru. I know what sort of battles you've endured... Poverty, prison, crack and cancer... Through it all, you overcame, you persevered. Despite your yesterday, you smiled today and still remain optimistic about tomorrow... Life gave you lemons -you've made lemonade... and for that, I couldn't possibly be any more proud of you.

For the record, Ma, I was almost in tears today when we spoke. You almost had me... Something about a mother's tears- they move even the hardest men... *I Love You Ma* ... and I'm proud of you.

CHANGE: To be or cause to be different...

Change is inevitable - time changes, seasons change, circumstances change, feelings change... Flowers bloom, flowers die, the sun rises, the sun sets, beauty fades... Change is essential - Without it there can be no growth, improvement, progress... Without change we cannot rise above our current situation, we can't triumph over our present battle... Our culture is changin... technology is changing... Social media is alterin every aspect of our lives...

So, old man, why are you stuck in your old ways? Staunchly refusin to accept the world as it is, futilely longin for the old days? Why are you stubbornly attemptin to hold on to an era that has long abandoned you, like tryin to hold water as it slips through your fingers? Until you become bitter and resentful, lookin with disdain upon a world that you've allowed to render you obsolete? And all you can say to justify your folly is, *"This is just who I am"*...

Young man, surely you don't mean it when you say, *"I ain't gon' neva change"*. Who has deceived you into believin you are exempt from succumbin to the same fate as everyone around you and all those who've lived and died before you? Young man, unless you meet your Maker early, you too will be old... Your strength will wane, your swagger will ebb, your passions will subside, your worldview will evolve... You see, there is no stasis in life's system and cycle... *YOU MUST CHANGE!!!* *You* have no say in that matter. What you do have control over, however, is how you change... You can *evolve* or *devolve*. You can *progress* or *regress*... You can be the catalyst that effects positive change, or you can allow change to effect negatively upon you... Don't *fear* change... *Embrace* it, *Welcome* it!!! Because none of us can *Avoid it*...

5/17/14

Back in the Days

I miss them summer days in southern Florida... When I could smother stomach pangs a hundred ways with just a quarter... Lilly-dillies, nutty-buddies, pickled sausage, pickled eggs... Moon-pies, star-crunch, grape sodas, all boot-leg... No shoes, no shirt, no father, no worries... no school, no sense ofttimes, no curfew, no hurry... Unfettered by feelin's of inadequacy or compulsion toward accomplishments. Pocket lent, not a cent, just a snotty-nose with uncommon sense... Simon says, hopscotch, or workin' on my handstand... Granddaddy in wife-beater and suspenders, overseein' our endeavors, mouth full of Redman... Stone crabs, sugar-cane, watermelon, catfish... Box-spring and a mattress, ghetto trampoline, doin' back-flips... Reckless abandon... Unaware of the fact that I was neglected and abandoned...Spam and corned beef hash from meals on wheels kept us from famine... Oblivious to the reality of the extent to which addiction and poverty infected and disconnected my family... Life switched, from light to dark, like a light switch...

Struck out swingin' with all my might at life's pitch... A picture's worth a thousand words, but the right words are priceless... I've done so much wrong, all that's left is to write it Went from back-to-schools woes, worryin' about new clothes... To razor-wire, C/Os, brogains, and blue clothes... No new friends - only new foes... Hard to let go of the past, when only God knows what the future holds..... I use to throw away scuffed shoes, now I'm sewin up shoe soles... Our justice system's injustices got my partnaz searchin' for loopholes... Crucial- I've had it all the way up to where the noose goes...

May 23rd, 2014

"What Would U Attempt 2 Do, If You Knew U Could Not Fail?"

7/5/13

What is failure? Failure can be a blessing, or a curse... Or, rather the FEAR OF FAILURE, can be blessing or curse... FEAR CAN BE A MOTIVATOR ... Meaning, the fear of failure can become the very driving force that propels us to greater heights... Fearing failure motivates you to succeed... TO GO HARD!! It can be the fire that burns within us, causing us to discipline ourselves, to sacrifice, to remain diligent in the face of adversity...

When a person determines that failure is not an option - that they must SUCCEED OR DIE TRYING... SUCCESS OR DEATH... Almost anything is possible... Fighters, Athletes, Warriors... They all fear failure... That's the fuel that makes their fire burn... That's what compels them to be great... For a warrior, failure could mean no more chances to succeed... There aren't many things in life that can drive us more than the FEAR OF FAILURE ... So, the question is: "WHEN YOU KNOW FAILURE IS POSSIBLE, WHAT ARE YOU WILLING TO DO TO AVOID IT?" HOW FAR ARE YOU WILLING TO GO, WHEN FAILURE ISNT OPTIONAL?

But, hold on; there's more... There's the curse-side of the coin... FEAR OF FAILURE CAN CLIP OUR WINGS...

Meaning, sometimes the fear of failure can be a crippling element, that keeps us from trying...cause the FEAR OF FAILING OUTWEIGHS THE JOYS OF SUCCESS. So, rather than believing we can fly, we stay grounded, cause it's less risky...

Imagine a baby, learning to walk... They stand up, and they fall... They stand, take one step, and they fall... They take two steps, and they fall... And they get tired of bruising their backside, and decide they're going to give up on walking... CAUSE THE PAIN OF FALLIN OUTWEIGHS THE PLEASURE OF WALKING... So, they give up on walking & content themselves with crawling... It's the same in life, and in love... FEAR OF HEARTBREAKS HINDERS OUR ABILITY TO LOVE... FEAR OF FAILURE HINDERS OUR ABILITY TO TRY... So, my question to people like this is: "WHAT IS FEAR OF FAILURE PREVENTING YOU FROM ATTEMPTING?" That's the real question, which will also answer the original questions... MY ANSWER IS...

"IF MY DESIRE TO SUCCEED IS GREATER THAN MY FEAR OF FAILURE... I'll TRY ANYTHING ..."

"Da Alphabet Man"

I observe him daily, as he engages in various activities... All of the activities futile, none of them productive or conducive toward success... THINKING INSIDE THE BOX... A statistic, a victim of himself... Content in his failure... No <u>future.</u> spending his <u>present</u> stuck in his <u>past</u>... Which is the same as his present and sadly, just like his future...

I use to adamantly, vehemently, argue that no one deserves to spend their lives in prison... That was before I met THE ALPHABET MAN... I've met dozens now, and though the names are different, the letters on the ID tell the same story...

By ALPHABET MAN, I mean the individual who has had his right to be free - one of our most basic, primitive rights - snatched away... Who has been a victim of oppression, who has been told what to wear, where to sleep, when to eat, what to eat... Who has been a victim of humiliation, who has had to endure demoralizing, degrading circumstances... Who has longed for the touch and intimacy of a woman, yet been deprived of it... who has been chained, and shackled, and shipped, and forced into labor like a slave... Who has been caged like an animal... Longing for liberty, yearning to be free!!!

And who has had his most fervent prayers for freedom answered... Who has been emancipated and restored to humanity... Only to exchange that freedom for bondage again... and again... and again... Each time, earning another letter of the alphabet that symbolizes his most recent failure...

A...B...C...D...F...G...H...I...J...K... and the saga continues... The story drags on, like a sad song stuck on repeat...

His life, his presence, his existence, his story, his failures... They spit in the face of every man fighting for his freedom... Every man studying law, searching for loop-hole, waiting on appeal, praying for a blessing... Every man who made that life-changing decision that resulted in a life sentence... Every man living with the fear of never taking another breath of freedom... Every man hoping against all odds...

But THE ALPHABET MAN serves a purpose, whether he knows it, or not ... He serves as the ANTITHESIS of everything I believe, everything I stand for, everything I strive for... The very fact that he has thrown the towel in on life, inspires me to stand... ALPHABET MAN, you're my REVERSE ROLE-MODEL... You inspire me to GO HARD!!! Keep leading by example, and I'm keep doing the exact opposite... Keep FAILING cause in your FAILURES, you're inadvertently showing me what I gotta do to SUCCEED...

My God is Too Big for Your Closet!!

Those of you who call yourselves liberals, or free spirits have done all your deeds in secret, behind closed doors. You, who prefer darkness and despise light, because it illuminates your taboo, deviant lifestyles. You, who have spent your lives lurking and dwelling in the shadows, because your deeds are too unspeakable and reproachful to be done openly. You, who tell children they can no longer pray audibly in school, who have removed the most vital 2 words (Under God) from your nation's pledge, and teach evolution's lies in your textbooks. You, who have removed the ten commandments (The Original Law) from your courthouses, and in those very same courthouses, legalize homosexual marriages, or "civil union"... You, who condemn soldiers (Whom you've placed in death's clutches, in the name of patriotism) for sharing their faith in life after death, yet laud Jason Collins as 2013's Jackie Robinson for "coming out" as America's first openly gay NBA player. You, who murder unborn and partially born children, in the name of freedom of choice...

You, who are constantly, slowly emerging from the darkness of your closets, and in the process, attempting to force men of faith, men of honor, men of God into those very same closets... NEWS FLASH: MY GOD IS TOO BIG FOR YOUR CLOSETS!!! You cannot close Him in or tune Him out! You cannot sweep Him under a rug! You cannot omit the Omnipresent, Omnipotent, Alpha and Omega!!! You cannot force Him into your closet!!! MY GOD IS TOO BIG FOR YOUR CLOSET!!!!

6/5/13

Poetry in Motion

Poetry in motion... Words floating continually in a vast sea of emotions... Thoughts drifting in the open sky, coasting... Spilling forth, like champagne when it's lifted high, toasting... Poetry is the result of a soul that needs to be heard... And that soul finds expression when it bleeds into words... Words that invoke, inspire, and intrigue when they're heard... Poetry is, by definition, life that is written... Raw emotions and concepts polished by repetition, conveyed in high definition... To a receptive audience, who has the ears to see and eyes that will listen...Who can view another's art from their own perspective, and not despise the others vision... Poetry is writing your wrongs, your rights, your struggles, your sorrows...

Yesterday's lessons, thoughts of today, hope for tomorrow... Beauty, pain, scars, tears and laughter... Love, hate, desire, failure, triumph, all captured... Poetry is life in motion.

7/11/13 11:29pm

Inmate

There is great significance in a name. In the days of old, a person's name was consistent with their physical, emotional, mental, or spiritual characteristics... A person's name was their _Identity_. In prison, one of the primary objectives of the officials is to strip you of your _identity_... Rather than address you on an individual basis - by our name - they call you _inmate_...

Notice the spelling of the word _INMATE_... Keep in mind their goal of robbing you of your _identity_, and that your _name_ is your _identity_. If you take the _N-M-A-E_ away from Inmate, all that remains is I-T... If you remove the _NAME_ from the _INMATE_. all that remains is an _IT_.

_IT_ is a pronoun used to describe "A non-human entity, an animal. Or a human whose sex is unknown or irrelevant..." _IT_ also describes an _INANIMATE_ object... _INANIMATE_ means not alive, not real, not human. Notice the spelling of _INANIMATE_ ...I + _ANINMATE_, by switching the positioning of the first two vowels and consonants, creates the word _INANIMATE_ ... So, when I become _AN INM ATE_, to the officials, I become an _IT_... An animal, a non-human.

They dehumanize us because, to many, we aren't human... They call us _INMATE_ because, to them, we have no identity... Our name is irrelevant... They take an INMATE's _NAME_, and reduce him to an _IT_. A non-human entity, an animal, an inanimate object... Your dreams, your values, your opinion, your life means nothing here. Your sense of self is being smothered... There is a lot in a *NAME.*

In the Bible (The book of Daniel}, there is a story of four men. *Daniel, Hannaniah. Azariah.* and *Mishael* ... Each of their names have significance. *Daniel*= "My God is My Judge". *Hannaniah* = "Yahweh is Gracious". And *Azariah* = "Yahweh Has Helped".

These four men of God, Hebrews, were taken captive by the king of Babylon. The were carried into a new land, taught new customs, expected to worship new gods, and were even given new names...

Daniel became *Belteshezzar. Hannaniah, Azariah,* and *Mishoel* became *Shardach, Meshach,* and *Abednego.*

Their identities were stripped away, their names were changed. Babylonians tried to enforce their rules, their customs, and their false gods upon them... But *Belteshezzar, Shadrach, Meshach,* and *Abednego* they knew who they truly were!!! They were *Daniel, Hannaniah, Azariah,* and *Mishoel.* They remembered who they were, and who God is...

As captives, in captivity... As *INMATES,* it is easy to forget who you are, and who God is... Its easy to adapt to your environment and adopt the customs, the habits, the lifestyles of the land around you... To answer to new names, to lose our identity, to forsake your God. As *INMATES,* it's easy to lose our *NAME* and become an *IT*... Less than human, animals... Remember who you are! Do not get lost in this foreign land, or allow the enemy to rob you of your identity... We are men with dreams, with stories, with emotions... We feel, we love, we are individuals, we have an identity, a name!!! Remember, there is a lot in **a *NAME.***

5/25/14

I Will Live

We've been sentenced to oblivion; to the land of forgetfulness we've been sent. Never knew I would personally experience this saying, when I first heard it, nor that I would so thoroughly learn it at Hard Knock University. And now I'm remembering better times with old friends. The ones who promised to be there till the end. Yet, their word they kept, in a sense. Which "end" was never clarified back then. For all I know, it turned out exactly as they meant: "I'll be there so long as it is convenient" … But do these former friends also think back on those better days that are all I have left? Do they recall them with tenderness, or bitterness? Do they replay those memories of those days in the stillness of the night as often as I do? And, what if I knew?! Would that knowledge somehow ease the unsupportable weight of the loneliness caused by their absence from my life? Would it compensate for their enduring silence? Will it fill the void? Will this knowledge demand that I also forget and move on? Move on to what?! But how can I forget? How can I deny who I was, how I lived and where I have been? Those friends are all witnesses of those moments we shared – the good, the bad, the indifferent. It is not as if, by our mutual forgetting, we could bring about the result that our past never happened.

I will not forget. I would rather remember those past days as often as I can, and thereby relive them again. "Recordar es vivir otra ves" (to remember is to live anew). So in the dark nights, when the weight of the present is heavy upon, and the alienation threatens to consume me, I will push against the darkness, and remember that I have lived. I will live.

W.R.

You've Forgotten Me
and It's Killing Me

I got locked up... You came up, and forgot "US"... How could you, after all we've been through?! Baby Boo got issues...Like those Jimmy Choo's shoes could have fed me for a month! But you'd rather stunt tryna be a player, and be a friend... I can't pretend... It bothered me, hitting rock bottom... Only to look up and see you rocking red bottoms... That money spent for the thrill of, "hey look at my new shoes" could have solved some of my problems... But I'm quite sure you have some problems of your own...So I hold my own, not knowing what to call home...So I don't call or write, thinking you'll miss me if you don't hear from me... And as pretty as you are, I'm starting to see that maybe the Maybelline... Was literally a cover up, make up and make believe... Probably got you thinking your greatest asset is your butt, but I ain't mad, cuz I'm your greatest liability... And the reality is, you've forgotten me, and its killing me...

Echo

Salute to Riders

First and foremost, I think we owe a moment of silence... to the women in our lives, doing our time right beside us... Us being the men, we never know how much you go through... Cause, you, being the women, never tell us all you go through... Silently bearing your burdens and helping with carrying ours... Voluntarily placing your hearts behind bars... And even though I'm in chains, you make me spread my wings... I swear, you're the reason that this caged bird sings... When I'm all alone at night, staring at my cell wall... Nothing comforts me, like hearing my name during mail-call... Accompanied by the fragrance of your perfume... Baby, you're too good to me, I swear I don't deserve you... Every single night you're home, waiting on a call from me... They ship me all away across the state, and you follow me... You give me your all, even though you can't have all of me ... So I put you on pedestal for all to see...

Mr. President

Mr. "Audacity of Hope"... I'm starting to feel like that was just a joke, or... Perhaps, an elaborate hoax, to ... Portray an image like the blacks are in control, or... Perhaps, the blacks are just so outta control, that... Them folks used a so-called "black" to get control back... You a puppet on a string... Promised us change, and we ain't seen a thing... Except more rights for homosexuals and more lax laws on abortion... And maybe you dividing the American pie, so immigrants can get them a portion... In 08', you got my grandparents all psyched and hyped up... For change, knowing you couldn't back all the hype up... "It's time for change" was your favorite line... I remember thinking, "don't he know change takes time?" And Trayvon's murder is the focus of the nation... Shining the spotlight on racial hatred and discrimination... And the stand your ground law is being stretched to include chases and false accusations... I'd like to know your position - or would it not be a good look in terms of public relations?

You just like the other 43 before you... Betraying and deceiving the patriots who adore you... and to think that I use to be "for" you... Now the only "change" is my attitude toward you... Mr. President

Maya

Today was the day the Maya Angelou died... The caged bird sang its freedom song, while the doves cried... Two days ago, "E" gave me a word from the wise... Then, yesterday, departed without saying goodbye... Prison weaves lives together, like threads in a sweater... Bonds and brotherhoods are formed, then inevitably severed...

But, isn't life the same..? Doesn't the free man experience loss, just like the man in stripes and chains..? Shouldn't death be viewed as respite from pain..? Who is to be pitied- he who dies, or he whose life remains..? Maya's body retired from old age... Now, her spirit soars on the wings of eternity- no cage... Embracing the emancipation that she longed for... Living in the liberty the caged bird sang her song for ... Assuming she avoided entering eternity through the wrong door... For, Heaven's Long Shores are the lone reward worth enduring the world's wrongs for ...

Cold world; rare sunshine, plenty rain, all kinds of thunder... Upper-class perishing with greed - lower class dying from hunger... Old folks running outta time -young folks trying to give back the time they're under... We're asleep on our youth, at the absolute WORST time for slumber... I speak the truth, though you wouldn't believe unless it was succeeded by signs and wonders... Evil is ever-seeking to divide and conquer, and "We the People" are weak, feeble and prime for plunder... Blind, dumb, and deaf to the voices of reason... Screaming and pleading, until we're wheezing... Throats raw, lungs bleeding, souls grieving for lost... Young heathens running wild, robbing, killing, thieving, and don't even know the cost... The spiritual battle is *real,* and... The enemy, the lion is roaming the *battle-field,* in... Search of the type of cadaver *meal...He* can dissect and devour, and *still* ... We neglect and reject the power freely offered to the least and the lowest, from the *Most High...* I am just a lone voice crying in the wilderness, trying but they're not hearing, and only God... *Knows... Why...*

5/29/14

She Grew on Me

I gotta admit; she didn't impress me, at first... I mean, looking from the surface she left much to be desired... no exotic features, no glitz or glamour... nothing that jumped out at me or demanded my attention. I could've overlooked her.

But something drew me to her... and I don't mean like an incredible magnetic force... just a slight itch... the tiniest bit of curiosity... a "what if" ... the possibility of there being more to her than meets the eye intrigued me...

So, I approached her, slowly at first... without much enthusiasm, with very few expectations... and at first, she wasn't any more impressive inside, than out... Or, rather, I had a flaw in my perception, that hindered my ability to see her true potential or recognize her worth...

Something changed... time passed, and I discovered that, if I was willing to invest the time and energy in her, she could be rewarding, beyond my wildest dreams... I realized how truly beautiful she is... She's shown me incredible depth, a willingness to entertain my most eccentric thoughts, and unparalleled capacity to listen without judgement... The more I pour into her, the more she gives back.

I love her in a way I never imagined possible... I've come to rely on her presence in my life... I share everything with her... I don't know how I did it without her all these years... she's taught me so much!! She's taught me that it's what's on the inside that makes you truly beautiful...

She's also taught me that "you can't judge a book by its cover". So, in closing, journal, baby, I'm glad I found you... I'm thankful for what we share and excited to see where it's headed... hopefully you, share my feelings, and want the same thing, cause I'm all in with you...

Twisted Justice

Justice gets twisted like dreads... No skittled rainbows projected in the projects... Dark hoodies in the hood - young "Trayvon" is dead... 16 hours of deliberation and the jury just read... "not guilty", no pity, no incarceration ahead... "Zimmerman's free on all charges... Never saw prison or experienced the heartaches of bondage... I'm sorry! I just want to go home, but I'm being held hostage... so exhausted of promises, my thoughts mesh like collages... hoop dreams through my seed, I pray he hits college... cause right now he's balling... like "Denzel" and "Ray Allen", thank "Jesus". He Got Game like his father... here something for starters... I was never wild, nor a problem child, just a child with problems... for some I had answers and some I cheated to solve them... prison doors keep revolving... spiritually I'm evolving... reaching out to the reader, even though my conscience is my audience... You can't call yourself a leader if you haven't done a lil' following... "Abel" voice has been hollering... so why is everything so quiet? Isn't silence worse than violence? Where's the looting... where's the shooting and riots? "Can we dream?" It seems we can't - as if we're suffering from insomnia... By the way, forgive me your honor, but I don't honor your dogma... How do you trust in God, then hypocritically judge us... And did you read what Face wrote to "Obama"?! Barack is an actor so its only right Face gives him some drama... It was just a spec of what's considered politically incorrect... and I suspect that they'll neglect and let Egypt rip itself to shreds... them people serious in Syria, they over there cutting off heads... there's a river in Egypt we constantly tread in our heads... no more milk, no more honey. Just recipes from the book of the dead...

Can't you see the red sea flows from all the blood that's been shed... can't even structure sandcastles without the hassle from pharaohs or breaking some bread... the Feds got reserves so why is this nation in debt? It is so profound you might drown, so don't keep holding your breath... and lately I've been flirting with my future - I can't wait to get her in bed... I'm trying to brighten up her life so she can love me till death... Every time I think about her all I do is plan ahead... Because when it comes to my future, I don't know what to expect.

"Echo"

You Ever Feel?

You ever feel like nobody is really feelin' you? And your thoughts keep goin' over heads, like ceilin's do..? You ever get so fed up livin' amongst the dead, 'till its killin' you? But you gotta stay strong and hold it together - like, gorilla glue..? When, really you want to "act-a-baboon" like you're in a zoo..? You ever ventured outside the box, into the deep with no inner-tube..? In the Belly of the Beast, serving ya'II my life sentences... Waiting on a chance to spread my wings - coping thru the chrysalis... I use hip-hop to invest in the youth and draw their interest... While these dudes sit around with a hand up their rear - ventriloquists... And "E" has hopes of his seed stuntin' like his daddy on a ball team... I'm just praying for a seed - 28 with no offspring... I spring off topic at times, cluttered mind producing rugged work... Its no pressure, stay in your box and listen to me shovel dirt... Scars remind us that the past is real, and that the struggle hurts... But I fear no evil - faith in Jesus - no Shuttlesworth... If it wasn't for the dark, how could the stars shine?! My brightest thoughts emerge from the darkest recesses of my mind... And not all stars burn with the same intensity... Not all stars are All-stars -they don't burn with equal potential or propensities... So, I go harder than most - expend a little more energy... Because, love me or hate me - when I'm gone, they will remember me... The river in your head "E" mentioned results in stagnation... Because denial prevents many from pursuing their aspirations...

Gradually graduating from a river, into a Dead Sea... Where there is no progress, nothing lives, and nothing is set free... But my streams-of-consciousness *Flow,* like *Progressive... Insuring life* to those who get it - get it..? It will don on you in due time, if you let it ... I don't expect it; but if tomorrow's dawn comes, I'ma caress it ... Like the flesh of my newly-wed and - like a newborn - ask God to bless it ... For now, I'm just trying to appreciate my latest gift - The Present... Exit

7/15/14

August One

What's happenin', world? I'm your author here for August One... A son of August, born into the August sun... Lee Memorial, Fort Myers, Florida is where it all begun... When Bonnie met Elijah and they started vibin', all in fun... Hopin' they'd elope, she'd have a husband and a young'n, & call it done... But who knew my father would run? Leaving Bonnie stunned and shunned by all, to smother troubles with drugs and alcohol until it all went numb... Call it dumb, but neither one was ready for a son... I mean, they were all so young... Right? Nothin' poetic about it... Besides the fact that they produced a poet up out it... A brave-hearted Leo... With a razor-wire mind, and a flow that stays below zero... Who would use beats to free his people, although he's no hero... Just an overcomer from the gutter who refuses to believe all the answers to life's questions have to be "no"... That would be me, yo... The Face of Face Expressions... He whose ambition borders on a state of obsession... He who stays progressin', even in the face of oppression... & even though they stay assessin' and speculatin', I take it as a blessin' and keep pressin' on... Turnin' stumbling blocks into steppin'-stones... In essence, their hurdles provide pedestals I'm steppin' on... I rep the throne of the Most High God until my breath is gone... Pour my heart out to Him so much, my prayer closet is my second home... Because this place will drain you... & though we try to stay the same, the fact remains - *this place will change you* ... Even in August, you can grow cold here... Watching dudes die young and grow old here... Listenin' to all the schemes gettin' ran and all the lies bein' told here... Cards get pulled like weeds, and dudes get called out like roll - "Here!" & the saga unfolds here... Bullies get murdered and shanks make cowards bold here... Dudes speak in code, and do dirt under the c/o's nose here... Even in blues, we chase green - "Shrek-Mode" here... Relationships with women on the "outs" come and go here... Everybody takes some losses walkin' this road here... But the things I've gained are more precious than gold here... But I'm lettin' you go, so ya'll chill 'til the next episode, hear?

8/1/13

Happy Birthday Pt. 1

Adios 28, Hola 29... They said I'd be dead by 25, and that was close to true so many times... But they prophe-lied; I'm alive and well, and feeling fine... In my prime, getting better every year, like vintage wine... I'm on a mission, a sojourner of *The Truth*... Spiritual abolitionist like *Sojourner Truth*... This world is inadequate; it leaves much to be desired... We seek *Heaven* on *Earth,* as if such can be acquired... Beware of wolves in sheep attire... Who sell false dreams in their rush to be admired... It's so easy to deceive them... People are so eager to believe them... Even preachers mislead us... Guaranteeing we can be rid of sickness and free from diseases... If only we can glean enough faith to receive it... We conceal our flaws and deny our weakness... As if our pretense pleases *Jesus*... But he came for the broken, and I'm chief among those who fit the description... A misfit, spent most of my life just wanting to get in position... Father missing, life beat my mother into submission... I watched her struggling with addiction, suffering in prison... Battling cancer, which by God's grace, is in remission... Despite her issues, she still had that mother's intuition... She saw something in her son, through her drug-induced haze... She told me I'd become someone on of these days... I boxed and played ball-she never got to come to none of those games... No PTAs, no school plays... No watching me across a high school stage... There was only pain... Only rain... Only chains... Only thang on her mind was cocaine... And it wasn't gonna change... I grew up so ashamed... And what's really so insane, is I was almost the same... Going through growing pains... Smoking, snorting, popping, trying to cope in vain...

But I overcame, still overcoming… Living in a land, where people kill over nothing… Cold-blooded deeds give me chills in the summers… But the world keeps spinning like wheels on a hummer… So I don't shed tears over milk spilled in the supper… Not when there are still millions of children who hunger. My heart aches till my heart breaks… Watching youngins do the Harlem Shake, playing in the sand, making heart shapes… Till the waves of life crash down on them and wash their innocent art away… And they're caught up between drowning in life's deep waters, or becoming shark bait… Because we can't raise our kids-too busy raising card stakes… We gambling with our future, abusing our children, mishandling our future… Dismantling our youth… Disregarding our Creator, trampling the truth under our boots… So far, the results are a culture full of vultures… Cults, wars, surgeons altering sons into daughters… Meanwhile, I'm tryna pursue my destiny… Doing my best not to let the pressures get the best of me… In the refiner's fire, in a crucible where He's testing me… Spiritually I'm growing, expanding, intellectually… History, His-Story and irreducible complexities… Jesus was a revolutionary. And evolution's about as provable and truthful as the tooth-fairy… Yet, our schools carry it to students, who chew it like blueberries… Where are our values, is anything sacred, what do you cherish? Are you parents? If so, are you aware that whatever views you air, the youth parrots? Beware, in prayer that the damage can be minimized… Be a man that your family can epitomize… I'm 29, weight of the world on my shoulders, still I rise…

August 9th, 2014

Happy Birthday Pt. 2

Sitting here savoring the flavor of this delicious, mouth-watering B-day cake... You hear me? I said, I'm savoring the flavor of this delicious, mouth-watering B-day cake... Amazing how quickly The Lord alters our atmosphere... Enjoying a birthday celebration I never thought would happen here... Just last night, it was doubt, resentment, and an account without a nickel in it ... Today was cake, ice cream, buffalo wings on wraps with pickles in it... Yesterday was full of stress - today was truly blessed... In essence, I'm guessing the *blessing* came through the *test*...

So, is this what 28 is like? In terms of "station in life" I predicted greater heights... I mean, my station is so low, seems like it's afraid of heights... But because of unshakable faith in Christ-Who is the Truth, the Way, and the Light... I'm okay, I'm aight... & my spirit man has been on an exploration of heights... From the valley, to the mountain top, from the valley, to the mountain top... And I've learned there are things in the valley that can't be found at the mountain top... Hands down, the mountain top is the greater height... But the valley is where you go when you're chasing life... Its where the flowers bloom, and the streams flow... Where the grass is greener and the seeds grow... I was born in the bottom - raised in the gutter... Lotta cold nights and long days in the gutter... Many a day, I prayed to be saved from the gutter... Life headed rapidly down the drain like rain in a gutter... But I endured, overcame, and fought my way out... Lord, You sought me, You bought me, & You brought me way out... You keep me when the enemy tries to blot my name out... & there's a war within my members, so My Enemy is *ME*... & spirit man is willing, but my flesh is really weak... So my sins be as many as the fishes in the sea... But Your blood covers sin like foundation does blemishes on cheeks... But beauty's epidermis thin, while You're cleansing is Spirit deep... So, I'm in the valley, but the mountain's peak is within my reach... I'm living what I preach- I just hope that when I'm gone, they remember what I teach...

-8/9/13

Happy Birthday Bri
August 18th, 2013

Brione's B-day dedication, so I gotta dismantle this... Cut on the mic, cut off the cameras... Expect fireworks, although no gifts, cakes or candles lit... Only marks on calendars, to signify a little more distance between reality, and family... But Bri is no amateur- he can handle it... I miss ya, Boi... Its been far too long since I was witchya, Boy... I wish ya Boi could at least get a recent picture, Boi... Cuz, all I have are memories, covered under a decade of chains and fences... Haven't communicated with you in so long, I'm ashamed to mention... I could try to justify by providin' some lame pretenses... But the main issue is how much we both have changed, isn't it? Let's keep it real cuz we both real, and I'm a realist... We've grown apart over the years - I know you feel it like I feel it... We were born in the streets, so you're in the world, and you love it ... But I was born again after leaving the streets - now I'm *in* the world, but not *of* it... But we came from the same womb - we bleed the same blood... We slept in the same bed, bathed in the same tub... We shared clothes, we ate out of the same pots... Hustled on the same blocks, ran from the same cops... Not to mention, folks who tried to place us in a "home"... We went through the same struggle, though always together and never alone... We felt safer together thought it would remain that way forever... & in a sense, its true - we have a bond that could never be severed... But you're 29 today, I'm 28, & I haven't seen you since we were young... Time has a way of creating distance where there was none... But at the end of the day, blood is thicker than water...And despite our differences, what holds us together will always be stronger... I'm my brother's keeper- I will always love you, always be loyal... & even if I can always be there with you, I'll always be there for you... Cuz, I'm Baby Boi, and you're Brione... So happy B-day, Bruh - keep your head up and be strong... Won't be long from now, & we will both be home... We'll talk more when we're there... Until then, best wishes and sincere prayers...

These Pens

They make these pens... These razor-wire cages that they place us in... Where some officers sign up because their chances of making it anywhere else are paper thin... So they make their occupation incarcerating men... But the reward is far greater than compensation to them... They seek entertainment trying to break men who are trying to make amends... So when dramatic situations ain't taking place, they start creating them... Initiating confrontation & violating whatever space you in... Aggravating you, wearing your patience thin... "What, you want a new case? I suggest you stand there and take it then..." Some days it seems like these walls are caving in... & I don't know how much more I can take from them... So I grab my journal, and express the things I'd really like to say to them... Allow my emotions to paint the paper as the stress and anger escapes from within... Now, as if they know this is my oasis, they're working on taking our pens... No pressure - take 'em then... I still have a strong mind, loud voice, unbreakable spirit, and ain't no taking them... Ain't no stronger man than a praying man -Amen

-8/20/13

Self-Doubt

To those at a distance, I seem distant and indifferent... Mr-Nuthin'-Ever-Gets-him, the face of temperance... But beneath the placid surface exists a heap of active currents... I desire to plunge into the deep, but lack the courage... Afraid I might find Nessy... Scared to clean out my closet - things may get too messy... No one wants to air their dirty laundry when there are stains on the bedsheets... In our culture, men showing emotion is rare - like red meat... But everyone craves what may come next, and the table is set- so let's eat... My fear of failure is at its peak as we speak... Like 10,000 pounds of doubt at my feet, shackling me... The Devil has been after me, as a thief, tryna snatch my peace... I imagined it would eventually have to cease... But, after weeks its actually, gradually increased... I'm weak- unsure if I'm able to do what Christ asks of me... Its hard to fathom *He* would desire to use lil' ol' inadequate *me*... After 13 years in the Department of Corrections... In the *Mecca* of opposition and aggression... Enduring degradation and oppression... Deprivation and personality suppression... Being despised on every corner, dependent in every sense... Has hindered my development and threatened to render me irrelevant... I have a hard time submittn'... An even harder time committin'... In over a decade, I haven't made a significant decision without having to ask for permission... Aborting the mission seems more and more temptin'... Then, I look at my support system and I'm reminded the Lord is with me... "Lord, get me! You said you'd never forsake me! & I'm sore from swimmin', the waves are threatening to overtake me... So, take me, hold me, shape me, mold me... Keep me straight and focused... Too late in the game for faking - without Your Grace, I'm hopeless...

7/16/14

Sandy Hook Elementary School Massacre...

Which destroyed 26 lives, not including the devasted family members left to cope with the aftermath afterwards... 20 innocent children killed by one man... A young man who mental illness filled with ill will and transformed into a gunman... Whose rounds flew through that schoolhouse in Newtown Connecticut... Leaving our youth strewn around breathless - turning a peaceful community upside down and just wrecking it... Evil was the force to be reckoned with... At least it seemed to be, until we see the good that supporters met it with... A whole nation grieving, praying in agreement... An outpouring of love and consolation in their bereavement... I would never attempt to make light of the situation... But its my intent to shed light on our twisted nation... Something is amiss when we are distraught over 20 children dying violently in those rooms. Yet, dismiss without a moment's thought the many children dying silently in the womb... The first were precious and delicate flowers, on the verge of blossoming...

The second are seeds of life, just as valuable, every bit as promising... The first were crushed by violent hands - the second are trampled underfoot unconsciously... Both murderous methods should be equally appalling and astonishing... *Basically, if the parent loves the child, we as a people should do whatever we can to preserve the kid... But if the parent doesn't love the child, we agree with the parent that the child doesn't deserve to live...* When Sandy Hook hit us, the tragedy left us seething, outraged and astounded... But man look at us - We allow Sandy Hook to happen in abortion clinics, every day, all around us...

Whether folks disagree with Face, or label me... Regardless if its pre-k or prenatal, Face still sees a *baby* ... When the seed is sewn, and a fetus forms into a person with features, feet and arms... I believe we should keep that child from death and harm, with the same zeal as we perform after he or she is born... But we aren't obligated unless the baby leaves the hospital and reaches home... After all, the law enables it, so "to each his own"... America, like Moloch, to whom children were sacrificed, the beast has grown... And its leader Barack will give account in the afterlife for what he has condoned... I'm not saying a woman shouldn't have a choice of abortion or contraception ... I'm saying she should exercise that right of choice before sexual intercourse without protection... Casey Anthony faced trial for making a life, then later in life, allegedly taking a life... But if you make the life, and don't wait quite as late in life to take its life, that makes it right- amazing, right?! To women pregnant due to rape, I can't imagine how you feel, but there are still no exceptions... God makes no mistakes, and what you deem a curse, to someone else, would be a blessing... And us men ain't hesitating in every situation to claim we are man enough... But when we ain't ready for a baby, and the woman we been penetrating becomes impregnated, we ain't manning up... Blowing her off, giving her the cold shoulder, ignoring her calls...

Forcing her to make the decision of birth or abortion alone, w no remorse at all... Sometimes I wish The Lord would transport us back to before the *Fall*... And give us no choice at all, so we could avoid our flaws... Then death would be swept away-we could put a broom to the tomb... And our children would be kept safe, whether in the room or the womb...

7/19/14

To My Sister

Sis, I miss ya... Happy to get your picture... Wish I was there to kick it wit ya... Bear-hug Asher and plant some kisses on him... My lil "mini-me" - every spit his uncle... You - lookin' good, lookin' fly, do yo thang, girlfriend! Lovely as always- nothing changed on your end... I really didn't intend to go too hard w this... But I never should have started this if I wasn't gonna put my heart in it... Woman, I've watched you come a long way... Blossoming into Rose, pushing past enormous obstacles along the way... Remember them, "come-get-us-from-Copeland-rescue-us-from-our-mom" days..? Them, "me you-Brione-and-Juan -in-the-white-Nissan" days..? I remember when fate took Juan away... And though it may seem wrong to say - it was for the best, cuz he was leading you the wrong way... I've watched you struggle with your self-image because you're blind to your own beauty... You name it - I was there to witness while you were goin' thru it... Marriage, death, bankruptcy, insemination... Traveling across the state just to sit with me in visitation... Followin' your husband around the world as he is deployed to different stations... God answering your heart's cry- a naturally born miracle baby... So many different phases and stages... I've watched you display strength, prove loyalty, exhibit patience... Its been a while since we were separated by fences - eleven years... & close to 2 since I saw you, we vibed, shared struggles, expressed fears... I admit to having s little resentment-you've told me you've shed tears...

But it's a new day, and we each had to travel our own path to get here... You did your best and I did my best just to be where we are... & you're my S-I-S-T-E-R... & I'd give the heart out of my chest to keep you from being harmed... You've sacrificed, you've shown love, and you believe I'll be a star...Whether I do or not won't change the fact that you love me in spite of it all... That's why I love you and always will, no matter how the chips may fall... Your life has taken on a new direction, like *a flight change*... I admire how you balance the sister-mother-&-wife *thang*... I'll go to bat for you - despite whatever curves *life brangs*... I'm in your corner, like a fight trainer until I board that *"Night Train"*...

-8/26/13

We Shall Overcome!

We Shall Overcome! We shall Overcome!! The song, the anthem, the mantra of the oppressed... The prisoners, victims of circumstance, the homeless... Coping under loads so heavy, they cause soul stress... Yet, hope-full in situations that seem hope-less... Despite chains, determined to progress - Oh Yes!!!

We Shall Overcome!

The song resonates in my own chest... And though my bones groan in protest... I stand tall under the weight of a stone vest, cuz hope ain't gone yet ... And I know the darkest skies are where the brightest stars are shown best - Oh Yes!!!

We Shall Overcome!

You know why? Because overcomers stand tall and never lay down... And, even when we fall, we never stay down... Despite those that told us its over, we know its only begun... So, we press on through the night, into the morning sun... Lionheart beating to the rhythm of our ancestors' oldest drums... Voices hum and pour forth in accordance with the chords strummed and the chorus is sung - Oh Yes!!!!!!!!!

We Shall Overcome!

I Remember

I remember my very first taste of discrimination... Raised in the 80's - a product of a relationship that was interracial... In the South where it was considered, at best, indecent... For a Caucasian woman to be romantically involved with a man of African descent... So we sensed disapproving glares and condescending stares everywhere we went... Since my mere existence was offensive, I kept my 9 year old fists instinctively clenched in defense... Fighting vehemently for liberty in the midst of my oppression... Which, at the age of nine, came mostly in the form of ridicule, hurled ruthlessly by adolescents... I remember running, crying to my grandfather, who'd scoop me in his arms... Where I felt accepted and protected from rejection, hurt and harm... I remember he'd drown my fears in the melodies from his harmonica, while keeping time with his foot... and in that deep, rich bass voice, he'd sing those ol' gospel hooks... (Wade in the water... and swing low, sweet chariot, coming for to carry me home...) And in silence I'd sit, by the fire, transfixed as he played... His skin the blackest ebony- his hair the color of ivory with age... When he finished, he'd look down at me and say, "Joshuay, I remember... When I was just your age... When minorities were considered animals, barbarians, and incorrigible fools... Unworthy of worshipping in the same churches as whites or learning in the same schools - even swimming in the same pools... I remember struggling white-owned diners, would deny paying black customers a table upon which to eat... And on crowded busses tired ol black women were forced to stand on sore feet... While healthy young white men sat comfortably in their seats... Those who resisted or protested were beat - flesh torn open by teeth of beasts... On the leashes of police, who hosed them down in the streets... Young men were hung from trees, and little girls were bombed in churches by cowards hiding behind sheets... But, I remember!!! Oh, I remember something remarkable making it's way into the hearts and mind of the oppressed. The spirit of Rosa Parks that refused to move and sat in silent protest... The dream of Dr. King, awakening us to the reality that it was time to progress... The freedom song, springing forth from souls and spilling onto signs that professed;

"We Shall Overcome, We Shall Overcome, We Shall Overcome"

With the voices of a million ancestors echoing in his ears, I watched tears fall from my granddaddy's eyes... And when I asked him why he cried, he smiled with pride and said "because I remember!!!

See, my father was a slave's son, and he taught me where we came from... Ripped from our homeland and stripped of our native tongue. Babies torn from bosoms of mothers and wives stolen from husbands... Driven into a new land, given new names and new customs... They grew accustomed to being treated as mere pieces of property... Subjected to heinous crimes and unspeakable atrocities... Seems to me that, quite possibly, the single most shocking thing... Is... We survived!!! We sang our way through long days in the field... Took the scraps that were afforded us, and made them into meals... Even perfected some of the exquisite dishes for which black kitchens are best known... Collard greens, corn bread and neck bones... Ox tail, white rice and fresh corn... We were knocked down and stepped on, but got up and pressed on... Sights set on what was in store... Becoming pioneers and mentors, scientists and inventors... Actors and preachers, activists and teachers... Active in the game, and no longer just passive in the bleachers... Actually seen as, not necessarily stronger or weaker... But what we've been all along, and that's equal... We paid the price to change our plight and make things right... And thanks to white abolitionists and Freedom Riders who gave us the support and strength to fight... We've obtained our liberty, our dignity and our rights now... Represented in the Congress, the Supreme Court, and the White House... Yea, the past is long and dark, but things are different now... Our Ancestors freedom cries are mere whispers echoing in the distances now... We've overcome sorrow and defeat, and marched into triumph and victory now... Wounds have healed, scars have faded, it's history now... But I've written it down so that you and I REMEMBER.

BLACK HISTORY 2015
2/19/15

Long Suffering

I feel like I've lived 82 years inside these 28... Double portions of heartache and sorrow upon my dinner plate... Despite these prison gates, I refuse to allow myself to accept a prisoner's fate... Instead, converting failure into fire, learning to see the triumph in mistakes... Expressing my inner faith with the passion of protestors when they demonstrate... I refuse to lose - I'ma win it just for winning's sake... So that my testimony can be a template for success to those who're in this state... life throws curves no one could ever anticipate... Pressure makes pillars break... You either bend, or break - go with the eb and flow, learn to give and take... You will never make a *difference* until you understand what a *difference* being *different* makes... I have lived to be older than my past says I should... I have grown stronger and wiser than critics ever imagined I could... Through the tragedies life has thrown at me, I've stood... Ten toes down, chin up, back straight... Though I bear the weight of burdens that have historically made backs break... I paid my dues, plus inflation, never asked for a tax break... I'm entitled to backpay, but thus far, all I got is suffering in a lump sum, flat rate... But you reap what you sew and enjoy the perks of what you purchase... So, if I can see the blessings in the curses, and convert them into verses... That a person can interpret from my journal and be encouraged on their journey... Then the adversity was worth it, and the hurt served its purpose... life is a lazy servant - it only works if you work it ... Christ is the way, though sadly, He can't be found in some of the churches you're searching... If this Earth was picture perfect, there would be no bars, no chains, no wars, no pain... But in this broken world, we seek peace and harmony in vain... Being a warrior is in my veins... A title I've fought hard to maintain... No purple heart - my stripes are in the scars that remain... I do it all in the Son of the Virgin & the Carpenter's name...

Riddle Me This

You spend it, but never own it... Its borrowed, but you never loan it... It reveals history's mysteries, present proofs, and future prophecies... It is relentless, shows no remorse, and offers no apologies... It fades the boldest lines - it dims the brightest shines... It embraces *play, record,* and *fast forward-* but never *stop, pause,* or *rewind* ... It can be your biggest enemy, or it can be a dear friend... It has the power to heal, build, destroy, and build again... It greets you with a smile when you exit the womb... It bids you farewell when you enter the tomb... Abuse it and you'll hate - use it wisely and you'll love it... it governs us all - only God is above it ... Kings and kingdoms exist within the clutch of it... Some say they can never get enough, while others have too much of it...

7/8/14

The Crutch or The Cross??

Matthew 16:13-18

In my opinion, Christianity is divided into two distinct and polar categories... The Crutch & the Cross... Some draw a contrast between Religion & Relationship. I'll speak about the Crutch first...

We live in a broken world... We are broken people... Sinful, flawed, frail... Full of hopelessness, despair and depravity. We pursue pleasure in superficial thrills... We long for fulfillment, yet never lay hold of it... We seek love in all the wrong places... We have insatiable needs that we go to great lengths to satisfy... We yearn for Eternal Peace, yet remain in a constant state of unrest...

We use any means of escape, any coping methods, any crutches that seem to offer us reprieve from the immense burdens of life... We are constantly seeking, searching, and striving for the ever elusive answers to our problems...

Then, we hear the gospel of Jesus Christ... How he loves us, how he died to save us and to bestow upon us the free gift of Eternal Life, which ensures us a mansion on the streets of gold, walls of jasper... Eternal Rest of the weary soul. Healing for the wounded spirit... We even get to exchange imperfect, ailing, disease ridden bodies in heaven...

In our desperation, in our discontentment, and our desire to discover what has been missing in our lives... After trying to fill that void through drugs, sexual gratification, adrenaline rushes, only to come up short, again and again… We "give God a try…"

We've heard how He blesses His children – how He healed the sick, fed the poor, resurrected the dead…How He desires to give us a more Abundant Life… And that is exactly what we long for… We need lifestyle improvement… We need healing, finances, forgiveness, fulfillment… So we seek this Jesus, whom others say is the One who gives liberally to all who ask… Some say He is God, some say He's a Prophet… Some say He is just one Teacher of the countless religions of the world… But we have nothing to lose. All else has failed, and we need something, anything, anyone… Jesus appears to be our answer…

So we ask Him to come into our lives… To fix what's broken, to heal what is hurting, to restore ruined relationships, to undo what we've done, to do what we're unable to do… To break the chains, open the gates…to be our Comforter, our Savior, our Crutch…

Christianity: The Cross

Jesus said, "If anyone desires to come after me, let him deny himself, and take up his cross daily, and FOLLOW ME…"

Jesus did not come to *improve* our life… He came to *transform* it… He didn't come to make *everything better*… He came to make *"All Things New…"*

Peter left his nets…Levi left the receipt of customs… Jesus' Disciples left their homes, families, careers, customs, friends… Lives were drastically and permanently changed when Jesus called them…

Salvation exist in Christianity The Cross…When the Creator of the universe, the Sovereign, Omni-potent God of All Creation – by His grace and mercy, because of lovingkindness, according to His perfect will – *calls us*… He begins a regenerative work, a stirring of the inner-man, a quickening of the spirit... An awareness of our brokenness, a realization of our hopelessness, an acknowledging of our sinfulness, a thirst for His righteousness... A spiritual awakening and thirst that He instills in us... We come to Christ, not because we want more out of life, or because we seek external improvement, or because we need our next crutch... But because He calls us, out of darkness, into light... Because His Sheep hear His Voice...

And we answer... Because His call in unavoidable, because our brokenness is unbearable, because our sin is intolerable, because our thirst for Him is otherwise unquenchable; because our need is otherwise insatiable...

We respond to His voice by surrendering our will. By humbling ourselves, by turning away from our life, such as it was before we were called. By being Born Again... By denying ourselves, by Picking Up Our Cross... By surrendering to Christ as our Lord and Savior...

Crutch Christians attend church services, or listen to sermons because they need a word of encouragement...Because they need someone to reassure them that everything will be alright... Because they want to be a part of something bigger and more meaningful than themselves.... Because hearing a good message has a therapeutic quality that feeds the flickering flames of hope within them... Because being a Christian gives them a sense of identity and purpose... Because it helps them cope with the day-to-day pressures, failures, and demands... It's a Crutch...

Cross Christians realize we are the Church... And the gospel isn't to coddle or pamper or cater to us... It is the Word of God. We are the Children of God. We are here, in this broken world to be vessels of honor, and conduits through which Christ pours out His love and demonstrates His glory... We're to love the unlovable... To preach good tidings to the poor... To proclaim liberty to the captives, to be lanterns in this dark world we live in... To endure hardships, suffer persecution, to resist unto bloodshed, if called to...

Christianity The Religion provides a Crutch, for those who desire an *improved life*... Christianity The Relationship requires a Cross, for those who desire *Eternal Life*...

Christianity the Crutch can prove to provide nominal level of peace, to instill a vestige of hope, to lend a sense of identity... But the Crutch is a *Dead End*...

Christianity the Cross can prove to require exponential change, incredible sacrifice, intense persecution, increased hardship... But it is the *Road to Life*...

Christ can heal, He can feed, He can provide, He can comfort, He can restore, He can bestow... He gives Abundant Life... But *Life* is in *Christ*, not *Christianity*...Meaning life is not in the *Religion*, but the *Relationship*...Not in the *Crutch*, but the *Cross*...

What is Christianity to you?
Crutch or Cross?
Religion or Relationship?

July 10th, 2014

Fyrebrand

Religious Fyrebrand, political whistle - blower... Anvil droppin', Goliath slayin' lyrical missile thrower... Walkin' by faith, avoiding the land mines... Surrounded by 2 types - ventriloquists and pantomimes... The latter won't speak up - the former just voicing another man's lines... Teenage girls flushing babies down the toilet - *labor Pool*... Their baby-daddies smokin' K-2 like every day is 4/20 -*April Fools*...

Speaking of fools: The Young Money Barbie got your daughters on *Pills & Potions*... Drizzy busy sippin' syrup while he spills emotions... Weezy havin' seizures - whole world watching as the drugs kill him slowly... Celebrities air their dirty laundry on social media when they're feelin' lonely... Miley Cyrus clownin' - her career has become an ongoing circus... That 'Miley Virus" got all the flat booty girls bent over, tryna twerk it...

But, what do I know?... I'm just one of many rejects, with questionable precepts... Undeserving of society's respect... Cuz I'm an "ex-con", I been slept on like a pretest... Needless to say, I'ma press-on, its in my genes, like a seamstress... And, even though I need specs, I see through to the big picture, so miss me wit the pretext... Already causin' controversy and I ain't even free yet... But, if I had one wish, one request... I'd live for Christ and die wit no regrets...Some say I'm in too deep, but I'm just beginning to get my feet wet... In the valley, nowhere near my peak yet ... But if you think I won't reach it -you got me *Twisted*-Keith Sweat... I try to never let em see me sweat, but my clothes are covered in furnace soot... Cuz I am ablaze but not consumed, like the *Burning Bush*... More like, a ball of fire in The Messiah's hand... Or a microscopic ember, carried on the wind into the driest lands... To ignite a flame in the hearts of the vilest man, according to The Messiah's Plan... That's the vision, purpose and objective of a Fyrebrand...

-7/8/14

I·N·D·E·P·E·N·D·E·N·T

Do you know what that means..? That means dude is on the block, serving fiends, yellin' "C.R.E.A.M" ... Or behind bars, calling collect, sellin' dreams... Or, forsaking his queen, takin' leave to chase some little thang in her teens... Vacating his throne and his home... Leaving Baby Girl alone, on her own...

Wondering what piece of the puzzle she's missin'... Wondering what she's doing wrong, what she broke in their love, so she can fix it ... Wishin', she could go back to the beginning... Before the fights, lonely nights and other women... Spendin' her time between praying and reminiscin'... Believing she could win him back, if only she could get his attention... Long enough to make him listen, she could convince him...

Until she finally realizes she's trippin'... And tells herself she's sick of being a doormat and tire of being a victim... So she musters the strength to confront her fears and lack of confidence... Because, until now, being his lady and Baby Mama is her only accomplishment... Prominent among her fears is, she can't do it without him in her life beside her... Then, to her astonishment, something begins to come to life inside her... The Eye of the Tiger, got her singing Beyonce, "I'm a Survivor"... This is where the rubber meets the road, and she's a firestone tire... She's feeling inspired... Applies for a job, and to her surprise, gets hired... Her self-image increases, she's setting her sights higher... Her ambition is growing, along with her desires... She begins to acquire things for herself she only dreamed of prior... Men take notice - she goes from abused and misused, to pursued and admired... They sing her praises, make it known, put it in songs... How she pays her own way, how she's beautiful and strong... They begin to equate her "worth" with her "independence" ... Ironically, it is abandonment and necessity that gave birth to her independence... So, what am I saying? Its upon our failures that her success actually depends... *Independent women* are the result of *inadequate men*...

Hard to Say Goodbye

Why is it so hard to say goodbye to yesterday? Even though Tomorrow's sun rising over the horizon should take our breath away... What's behind us binds our mind until we miss the gift of our present day... *Lorde* knows, we'll never be *Royals*- we seek our thrills where peasants play... Every day, mistakes are made, lessons learned - bridges built, bridges burned... At times, we get more than we bargained for, often less than what we've earned... Sighing at the forked road... Tired of buying into lies that end up foreclosed... Even more so, watching poor souls dying over morsels... You can see the mire on my sore soles, smell the fire on my scorched clothes... I been through it - so don't judge me unless you are The Messiah, or wear a court robe... I been through courtrooms, cell blocks - I know how the story goes...

Attempted murder, kidnapping, carjacking, countless drugs either done or sold... But I don't revisit my past to brag or boast- I speak in *remorse code*... I'm in Reform mode... Right-handed - I write with the hand The Lord holds... I walk on the waves of life as the storm blows... Game tighter than cornrows... Life is a *"thorned rose"*... A stage upon which various actors perform roles... I don't conform though... I'm an outcast as far as the norm goes... I go where The Lord goes... I carry my sword - we're in a warzone... The battle is real, but victory is foretold... So, of course, I follow His orders, despite what the score shows...

Under pressure, never letting 'em see me sweat - pores closed... Point made, class dismissed, coarse closed...

Say, Church...

Say, Church – what it do? Tell me what the body is coming to, when you nonchalantly watch souls perish right in front of you... Shruggin' off abortion like is nothin' new – which, pretty much is true... Remember – Herod also slaughtered everyone under two... But nothing does the job like hot cars in summers do... And nothing screams abomination like gay marriage... & agencies allowing babies to be adopted by gay parents... The fact that we are destroying two of our nation's most sacred institutions is made apparent... Our children inherit sinful traits, and sexual aberrations become inherent... I'm praying for revival... But our nation is straying from the Bible... A generation with itching ears, they crave another idol... Tired of a living God, Who's holy standards and commandments only give 'em problems... They wanna be primped and coddled - sitting around all prim and proper... Watching men rush to their demise, and don't even attempt to stop 'em... If the lost think they had a grim beginning, the end will shock 'em... 3 billion souls waiting on us to commend to them the gospel... A feat we pretend is impossible... I contend that its feasible – though a tad bit colossal... Searching for a remnant in the valley of dry bones, I dig for fossils... Looking for *signs* of *life*... Trying to *shine* a *light* into darkened hearts, praying that *mine* is *right*... & the *timing* is *right*, to overcome my mountains, so I *climb* and *hike*... When I finally get *behind a mic*, I'ma *rhyme for Christ*... Lord, let me go out like Uriah – put me on the front *line to fight*... Even if it means leaving *behind a wife*... Until then, bring my Bethsheba into my *line of sight*... Let her be the wind beneath my wings, like *flying a kite*.. Cover us both in your blood, like when *lions fight*... Let your Word be a lamp unto our feet, and a *guiding light*... *Eternal Life* means I'll be alive tomorrow, even if I *die tonight*... My spirit and flesh war between the glory of death and the *pride of life*... Which just means I'm human; So I just keep it moving... *True Believers in Jesus* – it's not a label, partner, *we a movement*...

8/5/2014

Confinement

6:00am, class A, lights on, bed made... Pillow is hard, matt is flat, so I slept wrong and got a headache... Run-around is screaming "chow time" - State food on a wet tray... On my 11th day of the 21 it usually takes to investigate... I notice my bread's missing when I get my tray... C/O says its all I get today... I wanna snap, but I hesitate... Bow my head, take a deep breath & pray... Thank The Lord that I'm just a few steps away from better days... & its just May & its already hot like its summer... & I just ate, but already feeling the beginning stages of hunger... So tryna buy a lunch tray for 5 stamps becomes my mission... Along with tryna come up on a James Patterson novel, in exchange for a John Grisham... Dudes tryna trade k-2 for cigarettes so they under their doors "fishing"... With toothpaste tied onto ripped sheets - that "twack" got em tripping... Arguing, making death threats behind steel doors - I just listen... Until my mind drifts into a daydream, and before long, I'm reminiscing... That's when the stress comes... & I can't wait for mail call - man, I hope I get some... I write but they don't respond, like they don't hear me - guess they're deaf/dumb... It used to hurt, but after 12 years, you get numb... Okay, so I lied - it still hurts, just not as much... What do you expect? I'm outta sight, outta mind, and outta touch... & almost outta patience... Freedom, what's taking so long? I'm tired of waiting... 10 - that's what time they do master roster count... 9 - how many roaches I killed last night after lights out... 8 - the amount of stamps I'll have left if I buy this tray... 7 - number of peanut butter squeezes I used in the past 11 days... 6 - number of showers I've taken in the last 2 weeks... 5 - more days and Lord willing, I will be released - at least from confinement...

Well, I didn't get mail, & couldn't barter for a tray... Struck out twice, but oh well-tomorrow's another day...

-5/12/15

I Have a Dream

I close my eyes and all around me disappears... I escape the sights and sounds of my surroundings and my peers... To a dry place, where people are no longer drowning in their tears... Hounded by the years spent fettered and alone... Compounded by their fears of never going home... In my dream, I see Brione - powerful, provider and protector of his home... Bonnie is not a fiend - but a queen, sitting upon her throne... & I'm certain Nikki is truly happy when I see her smile... Making all the pain and hurt we've all endured worthwhile... In my dreams, my dreams are not dreams, but reality... I emerge from the belly of this greedy beast valiantly... *I Have a Dream* ... In my dream, we all know the Truth, and that Truth sets us free... There are no scales over our eyes, or veils that make us blind, because the Truth makes us see... *I Have a Dream...* That Dr. King, Jesus and the prophets' words never fell upon deaf ears or hardened hearts... But rather descended like burning embers into sinners and started sparks...

Illuminating the dark, stirring dead souls unto life... In my dream, I see a beautiful, virtuous woman - she's my soulmate, my wife... & my children play safely at my feet... Beyond the cares of the world, out of danger's reach... *I Have a Dream* ... Of a place with no regrets, no outcasts, no rejects... The old protect the young, and the young show respect... There are no unjust justice systems or overcrowded penitentiaries... No militaries, no cemeteries, or obituaries... There is no middle class, no upper or lower... Every belly is full - every cup runneth over... *I Have a Dream* - because I am a visionary... And I know the *Victory* comes after the *Struggle,* even in the dictionary... So, I hold fast to my dreams, for when I cease to dream, I cease to live... And only those who have awakened to such suffering as I understand the immense sense of freedom and hope that dreaming gives...

5/15/15

Scarred 4 Life...

3/7/16

It happens everywhere I go. I'm minding my business; going on my way, performing a task, in the middle of a conversation... Whatever... Lost in thought, preoccupied... and then it happens. I catch them.

They're staring at me with that curious, inquisitive look on their face. Whether the gawker is 6 or 60, male or female, black, white, Asian, it doesn't matter; the look is always the same. It's almost as though they're asking the same question with their eyes: "What happened?"

I'm often confused. I don't understand. Did I offend them? Do they know me? Should I recognize them? Do I have something on my face?

Then it clicks. Always within a matter of seconds, my mind registers the look... It's My Scar.

I have a 4 ½ - 5 inch scar that runs vertically along the right side of my temple... not a neat little razor slash either; it's a jagged, one of a kind, "what in the world happened?" type scar that even stands out among typical war wounds. Not just the length and width, but also the dark discoloration that makes it stand out, even against my already dark brown mulatto complexion. You can't miss it.

Most never ask, but some do. Many (actually, hundreds) over the years. "What happened?" My answer is usually more shocking (or perhaps, mysterious) than the scar itself...

"I Don't Know"

I really, honestly don't know. No one knows definitively. I mean, there has been speculation over the years... I was kicked in the face by a horse... I was the victim of some unknown hate crime perpetrated by racists, who were offended by my presence in their community... Both scenarios were explored extensively by doctors, although no agreement was reached. No one knows.

What I do know is that whatever occurred, it occurred when I was 2 - almost 3yrs old. So while I don't know <u>what</u> happened, I know <u>when, where,</u> and maybe even <u>why</u> it happened.

It was '87 & '88 when I was cared for by The Stuarts. They had a few children. Christian family. I'm not quite sure how they became acquainted with my mother or her struggle... Single mother, 2 boys ages 2 & 3, no home... No job, no car, no husband... No hope... Living in extreme poverty... No family to help out. Mother was an addict and would leave us with the Stuarts for long stretches of time, while she offered up her body (her only commodity) in exchange for any substance strong enough to provide a temporary "escape" from her otherwise inescapable reality.

It was during this time, while I was living (or staying) with the Stuarts that the "accident" happened. By "accident" I mean, according to Mrs Stuart, one minute I was playing, fine... Next minute, the entire right side of my face was opened. I never saw the Stuarts again. If I did, I was too young to remember. All I know is that, from my earliest memories, I've been <u>Scarred 4 Life</u>.

Only someone who lives with a physical deformity or disfiguration can understand what it was like for me growing up. Already the illegitimate child of a crack addict, growing up dirt poor, living off hand-outs, hand-me downs and meals on wheels... I had this huge, ugly scar dominating the entire right side of my face...

Even adults stare or do a double take. They ask who hurt me and my answer is always the same, "I don't know".

Children? Children are ruthless. It doesn't matter what happened or how it happened... It doesn't matter that it was beyond my control... All that mattered was that I was different. I didn't fit in... I stood out.

They stared, they pointed, they laughed, they joked, they called me names... I cried, I fought... I didn't understand.

Fast-forward to 2003... I'm 17yrs old. I'm in the County Jail, on the juvenile floor, being adjudicated as an adult... Consequences ensuing as a result of one botched escape attempt from the South West Florida Juvenile Detention Center, as well as an escape and car-jacking case in Hillsborough County. So, I'm sitting in the County facing prison time.

It's in County Jail where I "master-minded" my 3rd and final escape attempt. The first attempt was "botched" ... The second was "successful", though I inadvertently created another victim and was eventually recaptured. The third attempt was absolutely disastrous...

When it was all said and done, an officer was in the hospital... I was facing charges of attempted murder, escape, false imprisonment and depriving an officer of weapons and communication. My co-defendant had the same charges, though his included impersonating law enforcement because he wore the uniform through the jail during our attempt... I'm going somewhere with this...

While in solitary confinement, (where I remained for 15 months) waiting for trial, I began receiving mail from Mrs Stuart. During our correspondence, she conveyed a message to me, from a woman I did not know... The message was that she forgave me and was praying for me... I was confused... I didn't even really know Mrs Stuart, and she's telling me that a woman who is a complete stranger to me, forgives me... For what?! How could I have victimized a woman I didn't even know?! Her next letter answered that question.

This was the Mother of the Officer I had savagely attacked... and she forgives me ... and she is praying for <u>Me</u>.

Even though I was very young, and my mind was incredibly wild, misguided and lawless, I knew that this was significant... I knew that this woman, this stranger, this mother of my victim had every right to hate me... To want revenge... To be angry, bitter, resentful... But she forgave me and was praying for me...

So as I sat in my solitary confinement cell, all alone, at the age of 17... With felony charges mounted on top of me like football players in a dog pile... Facing life imprisonment, plus over a hundred years... No attorney... Multiple witnesses testifying against me in several different criminal cases, in which I was 100% guilty.

These 2 little old ladies were interceding on my behalf... one of which I'd victimized.

Now, I don't know all of the details... and there are areas I still need clarification in and blanks I need filled in... But this is what I know for sure.

These 2 Christian women were advocating on my behalf when no one else was... and when this Christian woman's son, whom I had done extensive harm to, had his chance at revenge... He chose not to take it ... He "didn't remember" the incident except in vague, general terms... He refused to directly implicate me, even as the State Attorney's office attempted to coach him to remembrance... Because of my victim's "lack of recollection" and lack of desire for revenge, I ended up with a 15-year sentence, as opposed to a life sentence plus...

So, you see... Forgiveness, faith, redemption, and prayerfully reconciliation are all present in this story... A story that began in 87-88, in Alva, Florida with a Christian family... and culminated 14-15 years later, in the County Jail...

I don't believe in coincidence. I believe in a sovereign God, who knows our end from our beginning... Who has predestined us to be extensions of his glory in the world... I believe He chose me, and because He chose me, He provided everything I needed to become the man He elected me to be... I believe every situation and event that has taken place in my life has ultimately worked for my good and His glory. I believe Mrs. Stuart and my victim's mother were instruments used by God to demonstrate grace, mercy and forgiveness in my life... So that my story would bear witness to His eminence, and be a testimony for those who are acquainted with it...

That is why I believe I was *Scarred 4 Life*... Regardless of the "what" or "how", I believe the "why" was so God could mark me... So that I would stand out... So that His amazing grace and loving kindness could not be overlooked or go unnoticed... My Savior highlighted me from my earliest memories, so that His glory would be revealed in my life...

And all the humiliation and ridicule is worthwhile... It makes sense... The Lord branded me as His own so that my life could attest to His love, His provision and His purpose... So that we could make sense of our suffering and take comfort in knowing that God has a plan and purpose, even for our pain... We may not see it or understand it, but it's working for our good... So it is my pleasure to be SCARRED *4* LIFE

Nightmare

I had a recurring dream as a child - a nightmare... Alone, engulfed in darkness so thick, I could neither see where I was, or where I was headed... I'd hear this blood-curdling scream for help: "Josh! Joshua, help me!" I would try to move in what I thought was the direction of the voice (I could never identify exactly who was screaming, though I knew viscerally that it was a loved one) only to discover I was unable to move... Like my legs were cemented... Like some unknown, unseen force was preventing me from running to aid my loved one. The cries would grow more urgent, more desperate! I would fight harder, struggle more! Until, eventually the screams came to an abrupt end, and I knew I was too late. I dreamt this dream several times, & each time, I failed to save my loved one... I never made it...

Watching my brother, my mother, my best friend being overtaken, while I'm restrained from going to their rescue... My childhood nightmare has become my adulthood reality... I'm living my nightmare...

5/17/16

Beasts of Burden

The strongest man I know couldn't bench 405 if his life depended on it... But he can carry on a conversation while standing under the staggering weight of a life sentence... He's remained upright despite shouldering the incomprehensibly colossal weight of a 42 year prison sentence... 21 of which were spent on death row, awaiting execution by method of the electric chair... Hoping against hope... Praying against what seemed to be his fate... Awaking every morning to the unwelcomed prospect of death, looming overhead, like an ominous cloud, threatening to unleash its contents and wash away his very existence. A man whose stride possesses a stoicism that belies the fact that he's endured loss after devastating loss... Witnessing the passing - no!!! That description is too light, too objective – "coping with the crushing blows" of losing his mother, his father and 5 siblings while simultaneously being confronted by his own mortality... His height is average, his frame is emaciated as a result of cancer causing him to have his stomach removed (another apparent death sentence) yet he stomachs more than men thrice his size... He is, to me, Job personified in the 21st century... And like Job, whose faith in God and strength of spirit capacitated him to endure inconceivable suffering, his story is a testimony of God's ability to equip average people to overcome enormous odds, and seemingly insurmountable obstacles.

Record holder in high school for scoring 42 points in a game, 42 years in the Dept of Corrections, 52 minutes from execution on death row...

and after it all, I don't see a convicted murderer... Nor a victim, a man to be pitied, a charity case...

I see a Titan. I see a man with tremendous courage and Herculean strength. I see a philanthropist, an altruist, a humanitarian who assists and inspires those whose own onerous plights have caused him to encounter.

Doug is one of many roses that have fought defiantly to push through the tiniest cracks in life's concrete. Redefining what is possible. Unsung heroes. Strongmen. Humble beasts. Beasts of Burden.

Beasts of Burden are those who exist under the burdens that seem, and in fact, are, impossible for the average man to endure... Men and women whose strength in adversity evokes awe in those who witness it... Because for every Doug, there are a thousand who have succumbed to the strain and been swallowed by the struggle... Precious few have reached the point of no return and managed to return on point...

But they exist. Somewhere, amid the sea of sorrowful souls bowed by the burdens on their backs... Amid those of whom the struggle has stripped away any sense of honor, remnant of dignity, or vestige of sanity... There are sprinkled about men of phenomenal faith, incredible intellect and supernatural strength... There are men like Doug. Tiny Titans, wrinkled withered warriors, gentle giants... And they are carrying the weight of the galaxy on their shoulders... They are Atlas, holding up the heavens... They are beasts...

They are: **Beasts of Burden**

5/5/16

"Cry of the Afflicted"

"Before I was afflicted, I went astray: but now I have kept Thy Word"
{Psalm 119:67}

The year was 1993. I was 20 years old, and been arrested for 1st degree murder, and conspiracy to commit 1st degree murder. I was told they would be seeking the death penalty. I laughed mockingly at this, though, because I did not think my crime warranted even second degree murder. Plus, I was overly optimistic. I grew up watching enough fairy tale movies, where the good guy always prevailed in the end - and you couldn't tell me I wasn't a good guy. Of course, I had killed someone, but he was a very evil person and he had made several deaths threats and had done many bad things to many people; but especially to me. So, in my overly optimistic mind, the truth would prevail, and many would see that I was actually a hero. I had killed the evil villain.

This, however, was not how things played out. Unbelievably, I was being portrayed as the villain, who had taken the life of a sweet, innocent young man, who had the world at his fingertips and a very bright future. What were these people smoking?!

I had grown up believing in God, but it was closer to a superstition. Since my mother was religious enough for the entire family, I was "in" with God. Being raised in a Catholic church didn't help things either. I was not seeking God, but I would not refuse his help.

Upon my arrival at the count jail, I was greeted by many men who had been getting acquainted with my case via the media. It only took a couple of weeks before I got into my first scuffle, at which time I was moved to a different pod. My new cellmate was a bit odd. At one point he started telling me that Jesus was coming back in 1994. I had never heard this before, but I had always been intrigued by apocalyptic stories. I asked where he was getting his info from. He started waving his Bible around saying, "Its all in there!"

This started me on a search through the Bible, looking for answers. I was actually surprised to discover that it was interesting. I had always been told it was boring. Plus, I would have assumed that, since church was so boring. The next thing that startled me was that it seemed to contradict the teachings of the Catholic Church. This prompted me to share this with my parents, who sent our priest to explain the contradictions. When the priest couldn't give me any logical answers, I felt inclined to read the whole Bible for myself to learn what it teaches.

Over the next few months, I started learning that God actually expected His followers to live a holy lifestyle. I definitely wanted God's help, but I was not willing to give up my sin. I had also started going to some of the services they have going on in the jail. According to some of these preachers and some of the guys in the jail, a person could ask God for anything and expect Him to do it. Now, I could do this. I would just pray for God to send me home, and I would make certain vows to go to church and read my Bible. I had always wanted my own genie. I give the orders and He performs. This was a relationship I was willing to have with God. I didn't want God, I just wanted things from Him. I didn't want Him to change me. I only wanted Him to change my circumstances.

What ended up happening was, I was *found guilty* and *sentenced to death*. That was like the opposite end of the spectrum of my prayers. However, I had read that God sometimes tests people before He blesses them. So, I was willing to go for the ride, if He was willing to bless me in the end. However, I started giving Him a lot of ultimatums. First, I should not be expected to do more than 5 years, total. I wanted a beautiful wife, and millions of dollars shortly after my release. I would remind God of the terms daily as I waited on *death row*.

When I arrived at my cell on *death row*, I felt like I had entered a horror movie. It was an eerie, dismal place. The walls were a pale green and the lighting wasn't very good. I continued to read my Bible every day and fall asleep praying every night. The days went by slow, seeing I didn't have a television or a radio for the first six months. I read a lot of novels during that time as well. I tried to put myself out of that cell mentally, as much as I could. I would daydream for hours of a different life.

After 6 months of this and other mentally taxing circumstances, I became miserable and really began questioning whether death row was my fate, or not... Had I deceived myself into thinking I couldn't possibly fall to such a fate?! I really didn't want to ride this ride any longer. I started praying that God would just kill me. I couldn't take the misery anymore. I had enough!

This went on for weeks, until one night, as I was praying, I heard God speak to my heart. He was calling me into a real relationship with Him, where He gave the orders, not me. That night, I opened my heart to receive what God was giving. I really had no clue what it was. I had been reading the Bible for years but had never understood the spiritual application of it.

The next morning, when I woke up, I had an incredible hunger for God's Word. Something was different. It wasn't the curiosity or obligation to fulfill a pact that had driven me to read the Bible in the past. What was even more astounding was that I actually understood the spiritual application of what I read, for the first time. Strange things were happening. I actually had conviction about sinning. I didn't want to use foul language anymore, as was my custom. In fact, there were so many things that I didn't want to do anymore, people started asking me if I was okay. I had a new desire for holiness. I had heard about "born again" people as a kid, but I thought that was a denomination, or even a cult. I had no clue that it was an *actual experience*, until I *actually experienced* it. This led me to want to share the good news with every person I knew - that God will actually come to live inside you.

My parents were very happy about the change, but others thought I went bonkers. However, I just keep sharing with them, even to this day

> "It is good for me that I was afflicted, that
> I might learn Your statutes."
> *(Pslam 119:71)*

After my "Great Awakening" in 1996, I found out that there were such things as study Bibles. I immediately had to have one. Over the next 2 years, I devoured that Bible, with all the notes and cross references.

In 1998 my sentence was commuted to life. As soon as I was released from *death row,* I found a chapel. Now I discovered something even more astounding - reference tools, especially Bible commentaries. I became an avid reader of commentary. I filled my locker with them, and I started hosting Bible studies in my cell. I started working I the chapel soon after, and I was involved in almost every single service, class, or Bible study.

In 2003, I was moved to a different prison. One thing that amazed me, when I first got off *death row* and met other Christians in the chapel, was that these other men also had similar experiences with God.

Now, at this new prison, there were many other men who were passionate about sharing the word with others. They were even preaching it on the rec yard. I immediately joined these men and fell into a rotation of preaching the good news. I quickly realized that some prisoners did not appreciate this. I continued though, regardless of some opposition.

Two years later, I was moved to another prison. I immediately looked for men who were holding services on the recreation yard. I was happy to find a group of men, who I quickly joined. We became even more organized, and many were encouraged through this ministry

I eventually started working in the chapel again and involved myself in more classes and studies. Since that time, I have learned Greek, Hebrew, and am currently learning Aramaic, have graduated a seminary program, and teach an assortment of classes in the chapel.

It has been 23 years now that I have been incarcerated, and 20 years since my new birth. I have come to learn in that time, that God uses affliction and suffering to shape the men and women who He will send into battle. The war is ongoing, and the battle is cruel.

I used to complain often to God because He has not yet delivered me, and I can still be heard some nights, crying out to Him, "How much longer, Oh Lord?!" However, I realize that His ways are perfect, and it is all for my good, and his glory. Yes, I still really want to go home, but I would rather have Jesus. I used to stress whether to file this or that, or just wait on God and be still, but over the years, I have learned to have a high view of the sovereignty of God

> *"Unless the Lord builds the house, those who built it labor in vain; It is in vain that you rise up early and go late to rest, eating the bread of anxious toil; for He gives to His beloved sleep"*
> *(Psalm 127:1-2}*

> I have rest for my weary soul. I find my rest in knowing
> that, "He knoweth the way that I take: when He
> hath tried me, I shall come forth as gold."
> (Job 23:10)

We all want to claim the blessings in the Bible as ours. We want to pray the prayer of Jabez, or follow in the steps of Daniel, David, or Moses, but forgot that God first used suffering to prepare His servants for the blessing. I have realized that God gives the orders, and His will *is* my command. He will grant me what He wills and withhold from me what He wills.

"The Lod giveth, and the Lord taketh away. Blessed
be the name of the Lord" (Job 1:21)

When the Church *in* America learns these vitals truths, then Christians will stand out from the rest of the world, and the sound of the gospel will go forth with the ring of freedom from the enslavement of selfish pursuits. In surrendering our rights to pursue our selfish interests and desires from others and the world around us (including God), we will discover *true freedom.*

"It is Good For Me That I Was Afflicted"

-**Marty P**

I Am A Disciple

"...Whoever desires to come after me, let him deny
himself, and take up his cross, and follow me"
~Jesus (Mark 8:34)

"Christianity, discipleship, eternal life requires more than repeating a
prayer, learning some scripture, and modifying your behavior... Eternal
life requires the death of life, as we know it..."

Today's Gospel has been watered down and custom fitted, to appeal to
the pragmatic needs of the masses... Today's Gospel has been modified
to accommodate our desires and needs... Christianity has become
the religion of tangible blessings... Churches have become luxurious
hangouts, and waiting rooms in which Christians wait to hold Christ to
his promises, and receive their reward... Christ himself is often reduced
to a genie-in-a-bottle, who is bound by his Word to grant us unlimited
wishes, and ensure us comfort, healing, prosperity, and restoration
of relationships we have destroyed... No wonder altar calls produce
dozens, hundreds, and thousands of mass-produced "Christians",
weekly across America...

"Most assuredly, I say to you, unless one is born
again, he cannot see the kingdom of God"
~Jesus (John 3:3)

We often read such passages without allowing the Holy Spirit to reveal
the magnitude of it's implications to us... Jesus never uttered on idle

word... He Is The Word!!! And He used an illustration of being Born Again...

When a child is born, it's mind is a blank slate. It knows nothing. It can neither speak, nor walk, nor think independently. It is completely dependent upon others. It cannot assimilate whole foods, until it's digestive system matures... It must rely upon caretakers for provision and protection...

Being Born Again requires the same process... The old nature must die (II Cor 5:17, Jn 12:24), in order for the new nature to exist. Before the Birth of the New Man, there must be a Death of Old Man... Old principles, old ideologies, old habits, old behaviors- must give way to the new... Being Born Again, requires learning how to walk, talk, think, and live, Spiritually, as newborns, desiring the milk of the Word. (1 Peter 2:2)

When Jesus calls a man - let me reiterate that; When *Jesus* calls a man - life, as that man knew it, is forever altered... You do not remain the same, when Jesus calls you... As Dietrich Bonhoeffer says in, The Cost of Discipleship, "when Christ calls a man, he bids him Come and die." Levi must leave the receipt of customs, and Peter his nets, in order to follow Jesus...

Not only must one die to self, he must "pick up his cross." The cross is an instrument of death and suffering... Jesus told us, warned us, assured us, promised us, that this road - that leads us to Eternal Life - would be marked by suffering, by persecution, by trials... This is the path that Jesus led by example, and the path His disciples are called to follow.

If this isn't the Gospel that's being preached, then it's not Jesus who is calling men. It's men, employing showmanship and charisma, to market the "Gospel", to generate numbers in attendance, membership, and finances...

It is often said, "Where there's a will, there's a way." I once heard someone say, "Where there's a will, there's usually a funeral." The latter is closer to the truth, or rather, closer to the Truth. Where there's a will, there must be a funeral... Meaning, when our will arises, it must be brought under subjection, to the will of Christ for our lives... We must die to self (Gal 2:20, Phil 1:20)

"It's one thing to die for Christ, and another thing to live for Christ"

I submit to you that dying for Christ is easier than truly living for Him... Dying for Christ requires one overt act... One decision, one moment, and it's over. Living for Christ requires you to consciously die daily. Constantly, continually, perpetually.... Dying for Christ requires one death - Living for Christ requires continual death of self. Period...

I follow Jesus, because He called me. He chose me. He foreknew, and predestined me. There will be no turning back. All I have, all I am is invested in Him. I've taken up my cross. I will follow. I will live for, and if need be, die for Christ. I AM A DISCIPLE!

Dodgeball Vs Catch...

I hosted a symposium on the topic of Effective Communication at Young Adult Mentor Movement (Y.A.M.M.) event held last night. There were approximately 75 men present, mostly young, mostly minorities, mostly high school dropouts, all convicted felons acquainted with the cultural linguistics common in the prison system. Given the reality that every man in attendance had lost the most important battle, argument, or debate of their lives when subjected to the judicial system, there existed a common communication phenomenon among almost all: A need to prove their point or impose their will in conversation... A need to be right, a need to win ...

I opened with an analogy I've termed Dodgeball vs. Catch... We discussed the essential elements of both, the bare necessities and established that they are the same: 2 People, 1 Ball. However, the objectives are drastically different. Thus, the entire atmosphere, the spirit of the games, are diametrically opposed to each other.

In Dodgeball, the objective is to throw the ball with such accuracy and velocity that your opponent is unable to catch it or avoid being hit and therefore, is defeated. Defensively, the objective is to avoid or deflect the ball thrown by your opponent. The atmosphere is competitive... In Dodgeball, the players exploit weaknesses in opponents, and the player with the greater skillset usually prevails... It's the nature of the game.

In Catch, the objective is to throw the ball in such a way that the person catching has the best chance to make the catch. Also, the one catching does his absolute best to receive what is being thrown. The atmosphere is connective... In Catch, skills are assessed, and adjustments are made to ensure enjoyment on both sides. No one loses. Both players win. There are conversational parallels...

Dodgeball Conversationalists are competitive communicators... They need to win. Every discussion is a debate, a word war, an intellectual sparring match against often unwilling participants... Dodgeball Conversationalists employ scriptures, statistics, and any "evidence" available that will bolster their argument or offer a competitive advantage. They're emotional, they interrupt, they dominate conversations, they keep score, they're virtually incapable of being objective. They need to win.

Catch Conversationalists are connective communicators... They understand that effective communication is a win/win... Every conversation is an opportunity to connect, to learn, to exchange, valuable ides, and to ultimately grow. Catch Conversationalists employ scriptures, stats, etc... For the purpose of enlightening, enriching, encouraging... Catch Conversationalists understand that it's a give and take, a pitch and catch of information and ideas... They take into account educational and conversational skill levels... Cultural differences, backgrounds, religions, socio-economic status, emotional state at the time of the conversation...

Words are powerful. Conversation is infinitely valuable. Those who are gifted with an ability to command any language should, with that ability, have a sense of obligation, to build and not destroy, to connect and not compete... To use communication as an instrument to build bridges and not burn them... To open doors and not close them... To play Catch, and not Dodgeball... Timing, presentation, subject matter, active listening, non-verbal cues are all skills that Catch Conversationalists master in order to maximize connectivity in communication... May we strive to leave Dodgeball communication to those in the legal and political arenas, while growing and advancing in the art of Catch Conversation.

Cooperating and not competing... Working together and not against. Playing Catch and not Dodgeball.

4/9/16

Divide & Conquer

Some scientists conducted an experiment. They placed 4 monkeys in a cage. Also, in the cage was a stairway, leading to an upper platform. On the platform, they placed fresh bananas.

Outside of the cage, scientists had a high-powered water-hose. They kept the monkeys in the cage, under 24-hour observation. Anytime one of the monkeys attempted to the climb the ladder, to reach the bananas, a scientist would unleash the high-powered hose on him, knocking him off the ladder, slamming him into the side of the cage. Leaving him terrified, confused, and soaked.

They then turned the hose on the other 3 monkeys, who had not attempted to get the bananas. They were punished as a group for an individual's actions. One made a mistake, and they all suffered the consequences. Over time, through repeated punishment, the scientists were- able to break the will of the monkeys. They quit striving for the bananas, because they learned the consequences were too great.

Once all 4 monkeys were thoroughly broken - when all 4 monkeys lived daily in the cage with fresh bananas that experience taught them weren't worth striving for - they moved one monkey out, and replaced it with a new monkey, who was ignorant to the rules. The new monkey would eventually become aware of the bananas and attempt to climb the ladder. In a panic, the other monkeys would attack him viciously... They would drag him down, for fear of the hose. Of course, the new monkey knew nothing of the hose, and had no idea why they attacked him. But every time, it was the same. Until he was also broken and quit striving.

The cycle continued. New monkeys were rotated in, old monkeys trained them and broke them in... Until the scientists no longer had need of the hose, and none of the monkeys in the cage had even seen the hose. Yet, the process continued. They attacked each other, keeping each other from striving. The first four monkeys were long gone, and the rest had no idea why they did what they did. "Its just the way things were".

Untitled

So much is transpiring. I exist within a realm of paradox, where life seems to happen at the speed of light, yet simultaneously stand still... Maybe its moving rapidly for those around me "in real time", while standing still for me, because I'm "doing time...

But I undergo radical changes as well... Some changes (i.e., my thinking, worldview, my spiritual walk) often occur suddenly and without warning. Some things - in terms of maturity- evolve slowly over extended periods of time...

"Falling" in the system at age 17 and being 27 creates a paradox of its own. I look in the mirror and see both the clean cut, fresh faced youngster, as well as the seasoned man with the receding hairline and premature grey hairs... I know I possess attributes of both. Some good, some bad...

But it's the world outside of me that seems to be changing drastically... Careers change, people become parents (often several times over), credit gets ruined, in and outta relationships... Life changes quickly. Surprisingly (and sadly), many of my 27, 28, 29 year-old peers still closely resemble the 17 year old peers I once knew... So, after 11 years, am I BEHIND or AHEAD of my peers? I guess it is a relative concept... A matter of perspective...

My comrade "E" inspired me to pick up my pen and get more thought on paper today. My journal could use some consistency... If she were my wife, she would have left me long ago for failing to value and cherish her, and spend time with her... But my journal is always here, always faithful... Always anxiously awaiting my return, as a bride welcomes her groom after a long journey. When I return, I usually have a gift for her - a precious gem or two ... At least that has been my Modus Operandi. I think its time to change the game plan... I'ma carry my baby with me on these journeys, and share each day's experience with her, in vivid detail - high definition, if you will... After all, life isn't about the definition, put the journey. And, after all, documenting my daily struggles, thoughts, ideas, experiences, and questions along this JOURNEY is the purpose of the JOURNAL... So, buckle up, world! We're gonna travel this road together and end up wherever it leads us...

5/31/13

Ode to a Young Writer!

Readin' your thoughts, I have some thoughts of my own... How can one be so young, yet so grown? I tip my hat and say, "rumble, young man, rumble! You have a gift-you'll go far- jus' stay humble, young man, humble! Carry the torch, grip it tight- please don't fumble, young man -don't fumble... Watch your step & walk light lest you stumble, cuz young men stumble... In this jungle, that we erroneously call the Dept. of Corrections... It can be Modern Day Slavery, with its many chains, and all kinds of oppression... Or, *The Crossroads,* where previously lost souls find their direction... Strengthened through adversity, wisened through lessons... To the naked eye a curse, though in disguise, it's a blessin'... In your own words- look where it's brought you! Look at what it's taught you! Look at what you've fought through! Who knows if you'd still be alive, had them folks not caught you! I'm not sayin it hasn't cost you - But the things you've gained are many, while the things you've lost few... So rumble, young man, rumble! Build your foundation upon a Rock that won't crumble... Fear God, love your neighbor, show your enemy compassion... Pursue wisdom, push your pen, learn to control your passions... Walk circumspect, calculate your steps, don't be "fastin"... Along with reading and writing, add some prayer and fastin'... All things in moderation... Remember world peace is more desirable than world domination... And it isn't the quick or the strong, but he who endures that wins the race... The journey is what's important, so take your time and set your pace... Stay grounded and down-to-earth, even when your talent is in outter-space ... I leave you as I found you, with much respect - Face

4/4/2016

Fear Not!

Feelin' like a lone warrior, facin' my giant... Calm before the storm, patient, defiant... Every warrior who came before me was defeated... So, I stand, knowing more than ever before, I am needed... But I was born for pressure, and this is my year... The Lord is my Shephard, whom shall I fear?! Know ye not in Whom I'm relyin'?! The Lion of Zion is behind me -who's this Goliath?! Who killed the bear with his bare hands - who slew the lion?! He Who has consistently delivered me from the midst of my enemies will give me the victory... I hear the voice of The Lord whisperin' "Fear Not! Be of courage, prepare your sling, I will give you a clear shot! So, your story will bring me glory from everyone within earshot! People from different nations and generations will remember Face, and *Fear Not!*" So, I stand facing this enemy giant... Poised vigilant, silent - though inwardly smiling... Clutching my sling, my stone is minutes from flying... Trusting Christ for its flight, for its Him who will guide it... More than all the battles behind, this battle will define me... When facing what lies before me, this battle will remind me... Never to lose heart, never to lose my nerve... And despite who opposes me, remember Who I serve... Though battles rage, my sword is heavy, my gear is hot... Remain ready, aim steady, and Fear Not... Though battles rage, your sword is heavy, your gear is hot... Remain ready, aim steady, and *Fear* Not!!!

4/6/16

Prison Cell Anemia

You probably won't find the term in an encyclopedia ... You can't google it, or find it on social media... Not sickle-cell - *Prison Cell Anemia...* A condition, in which *deficiency of hope* weakens ya...

Compounded by the manner in which these folks are treatin' you... Shacklin' and chainin' you - might as well put a leash on you... Smothering the human being in you, bringin' out the beast in you... Family abandonin' you, loved ones leavin' you... Or, perhaps they can't afford $2 a day to speak to you... Not to mention, gas money & traveling expenses for coming on the weekends and seein' you... Or maybe they can't stand seein' you... Knowin' all they see is pain - knowin' there's no peace in you... Maybe they can't stand leavin' you, behind, unable to take even a piece of you... with 'em... Tryna to be strong for you, so they don fake smiles that don't fit 'em... They have fears and questions about you in here, but won't admit 'em... So they've taken their most precious memories of you, and hid 'em... In a safe place, where they can remember you, with fondness and nostalgia ... Similar to you, reminiscin' with the pictures in your album... I wish I had a nickel for every prisoner who has shown me a sleeve... Of tattooed calendars, blowin' in the breeze... C/Os curse the air you breathe, but wouldn't bless you if you sneezed... Ol' men dyin' alone, when they could have been home, if only they'd taken pleas... Photos are eternal moments and temporary forevers... Mementos we cherish forever, and carry wherever... To share them whenever, we need to remind ourselves & others that we've lived, and we've loved... Been places and done things that are worthy to speak of... Because this disease - this *Prison Cell Anemia...*

Makes it hard for people to recognize your value, see your greatness, or believe in you... Society throws your past up in your face - they got bulimia... And you're stuck in this torment, coping with this prison cell... Anemia, where freedom is your only chance of getting' well...

6/6/16

Best in the Game

A young cat told me, when it comes to rap, he holds the title... When he discovered I write, we instantly became rivals... Like, we were the last two contestants on American Idol... He was chomping at the bit, I was like, "Whooa", pulling on his bridle... I told dude, I'm too old to be battlin' - I flow *soul food*. Food for thought - *spiritual tofu*... I'm young, but I'm old school... And I believe music is a door through which you share with the world what you go through. People appreciate my music because I come from the heart for 'em... The moment I start forming sentences to tear folks apart, its no longer an art form... Before that day comes, I'll just exit the art forum... People wanna know that you feelin' their struggle, and that you know that its hard for 'em... So spit somethin' heart-warmin'! Oh, you too hard for em?! Then lemme issue a harsh warnin'... The streets are dyin'... Younginz are killing in cold blood, mother's are cryin'... Little boys growing up accustomed to violence, clutchin' the iron, duckin' the sirens... Little girls on controlled substances *ridin'* before they old enough to be *drivin'*... Young generation of youth, thuggin' and wildin'... Old folks living in fear, duckin' and hidin'... Its *crunch-time*... Parents are serving dumb time. Children are becomin' young warriors on front lines, fallin' victim to gun crimes... Babies starvin' when it ought to be lunchtime... Darkness is fallin', the streets callin' for sunshine... & all you got offer is *punchlines?!* Metaphors, haikus, and hyperbolic soundbites?? But you the best in the game, right? That don't even sound right!! Learn to be fearless enough to spit from your spirit... So your peers can peer into your struggle when hearing your lyrics... Give 'em a piece of you in every piece you do... At least mention God, if it's the least you do... Stop lyin' in your lines, get some subject matter... Take some time out to rhyme bout the subjects that matter... Or-you can keep doin' what you're doin' & bein' what you're bein'... Another lost talent, who writes without speakin' and looks without seein'... Your court, your ball, your choice, your call... After all, you're the "Best in the Game..."

3/23/16

Otis

I risk coming off as a narcissist... By saying my artistry creates a sense of catharsis in the hearts of the audience who harkens it ... My passion for authoring the hardest bars is... Off the charts, partially a result the harshness of the bars behind which my artistry started... Until I'm dearly departed, and carted away... Buried, burned, or just tossed in a place for starving vultures to argue over parts of my carcass... I will continue to ardently tend to the sharpening... Of my pen, till I'm convinced its sharp enough to carve out a place among the sharpest men... Who have entered this art forum and left indelible marks on the target of history's greatest... Everything seems to get to me lately... Like, I've developed a hyper-sensitive nature... Growing immensely impatient... Some of my best years, spent pent up in cages... Dreams of ripping up stages dwindling away with... The only consolation being found by keeping my pen to the pages... & the occasional prison battle, blowing the competition away... But, I'm sittin' on the dock of this bay, watching precious time slippin' away! Oh, will I end up tragic, like Otis?! Who never reaped the fruit of the classic he wrote... Whose magnum opus was stagnant, and slept on until after he passed and his casket was closed... Or, I wonder if I will wake from this slumber... To come from under the rain & thunder... To rise above the storm & stand on top of the clouds... Looking down at raucous crowds, screaming obnoxiously loud... For the underdog, who emerged from obscurity, to burst on the scene... With verses as clean as detergent, tight as curve hugging jeans... With wordplay as mean as the serpent who deceived the girl in Eden... With his words, into believing things weren't as they seemed... & I can't rest, until I know without question... All my years behind corrections walls, honing my profession... & my obsession with my quest for perfection at least solidifies my place among excellence... I guess you could say, this is my last will and testament, to be read upon me exitin'... I'm out

-Exodus...
6/10/16

Analyze This:

Initially, I wasn't going to read the journal - just write in it - thinking I would be contaminating the authenticity of my direction if I read it first. Then I realized if the journal was to be successful in its purpose, reading it could only enhance my clarity, not corrupt it... After reading it my direction changed. Whether progressive or not, one's direction is often altered by the information and experiences one inhales. In this case, the paradigm shift was progressive. Instead of drawing on some profound data that my mind has stored from the past, waxing philosophic on some profound concept inspired by some great thinker who influenced me, or instead of writing something extracted from my mind's perception of who I intend to be in the future, projecting a visage of my mind based on where I envision it to be, as today's struggles strengthen me as I move into tomorrow... My mission is to attempt to allow the pen to bleed the simple truth as to where I am mentally and spiritually, right here, *IN THIS MOMENT* - Feb 22, 2016, Tues@ 7:49 am... Florida State penitentiary, Charlotte Correctional Institution.

I am by my birth name, Damian Daley. Based on the characteristics of my struggle history, the streets gave me the name "D-Nice". The transition spiritually caused the penitentiary matrix to rename me "Blessed" 17 years into a life sentence for murder. Parents were poor but driven. My dad was a pastor of Presbyterian denomination. My mother graduated college and went into the field of insurance. Dad pushed spiritual insurance - Mom pushed economic insurance.

I ran away from home as soon as I hit my teens. Running from the discipline of the well-structured home my parents provided. Two of the best parents a child could have, lived life suffering from the side effects of a *Prodigal Son*. I caught my first felonies at the age of 17. While doing a 4-year prison bid as a result of a robbery, *Mom hung herself.* My lifestyle strained their marriage and I strained her ability to find peace - a peace that heavily involved her being able to consider herself a good mother.

On the surface it would seem I gave you those details to spotlight my journey. On the contrary, I did it to highlight Face and his journey. I didn't intend to write about Face, and I struggled with the revelation when it came. Not wanting to endanger the authenticity of this work by writing anything that could be misinterpreted as a promotion of his virtues, just for the sake of. But I trust in the power of the Holy Spirit which is guiding this work - His presence in this work will influence its projection and reception.

I've known Face for less than a year. At one point we lived in the same dorm. (He was in cell 207, I was in 208). But we never had a conversation over 2 minutes. We first met in a college level theology class we were both enrolled in, but his journey resulted in him withdrawing from the class before we got acquainted. Both of our natures cause us to be cautiously strategic about who we embrace into our circle. Consequently, we just observed each other from a polite distance for months until he was moved out of the dorm to return to the program dorm (the dorm for men seeking a curriculum-based environment). We are both currently dorm leaders in the same dorm and our work in the youth program, in which we mentor the youth on the compound, has caused us to have to work in close mental and spiritual proximity to each other.

I say my following words in the *utmost humility.* One of the reasons they gave me the name "Blessed" is a God-given ability (that I neither initiated or strategically cultivated) to conceptualize complex thoughts and orate them with superlative fluidity. It is a gift partially injected into my being by a Dad who is a master communicator. I speak of these gifts not in self-promotion but in order to establish that I am not one to be easily bedazzled by gifted orators, whether they be philosophers, theologians, street disciples, chain-gang philosophers, I have encountered and out-debated many. So I speak from a conundrum of wide ranging experiences when I say, considering his childhood (which was the exact opposite of mine - thus, my purpose for sharing mine), and considering the savage environment of prison, where his maturation process unfolded, Face shouldn't be the straight up genius he's evolved into.

The son of a single, drug addicted prostitute parent, who had to hustle, who was sentenced to prison at age 17, citizen of some of the most violent prisons in Florida, shouldn't have made the transition from *gangster* to *man of God,* not in here, not in prison, not in the midst of an environment built to destroy the human spirit, to consume your hope and contaminate your faith. Half Black, half White, yea, you gotta fight in here to prove you ain't soft, and you got to be more savage and more violent to establish no one can take what's yours. With nothing but memories of having to hustle to survive, it is easy to fall into the drug deals. Its easy to make $1000-$2000 a week in here for dudes with elite minds. Income tax fraud can bring in $70k-$80k a year, with a cell phone, a support system outside, and an unlimited supply of social security numbers. So how does a man make a conscious decision to move beyond the prison lifestyle of hustling, that many used to position themselves to return to society with $100k to start their lives over? I watched Face do it.

Face didn't have my childhood. I have memories of a father who showed through example how a man faces adversity. Face didn't have memories of lessons "taught but rejected", only lessons of rejection. So when it was time to rebuild my life from prison, I had the foundation of my youth, as well as my dad to counsel with me during visits. My dad's pledge of financial support made it easier for me to leave the drugs and checks alone. Face had to make a leap of faith, making his transition even more amazing.

If you think this is a promo for Face, you are mistaken. This is a promotion of the power, mercy, grace, and omnipresence of Christ. It is a promotion of the divine and universal spiritual truth that, no matter how dark your life is, or how deep and painful your misery is... No matter how empty, painful and abuse filled your past is, no matter scarred and cold life has made your heart... No matter how emotionally and socially disconnected you feel... No matter how lost and hopeless you are, and how hopeless your life seems... The redeeming, regenerating, refreshing, resurrective, loving, enlightening, illuminating, re invigorating, redirecting power of Christ can touch you and your life! The transition Face made -from average to amazing, from lost to gifted, from follower to leader, from darkness to leading others to light - came only because he submitted, surrendered and accepted Christ into his life. Right here, in prison, inside this concrete jungle - *and jungle it is!* - in-the-midst of stabbings, rapes, racism, hate, drugs, poverty, misery and murder, the light of God shown through. God heard his prayer for help and responded to his cry. If God responded to Face in-the-midst of this level of darkness and despair in prison, He can, He will, He shall respond to you, in whatever hopeless state you think your life is in. God is waiting for you to ask Him into your life.

I was watching Face teaching a class, and I saw the young men in the class looking at him, wishing they were as gifted. I saw the older men looking at him, thinking how gifted they could've been, had they not squandered their youth running from God. God will empower you to shine for Him - *Christ!*

I took you on this journey so that every time you read Face's poetry or hear his music, you can now understand that you're witnessing a miracle. You are witnessing the unfolding of the life of a man who walked through the living graveyard known as prison. Witnessing a man who God allowed to walk on water as others drowned in the tears of regret based on past mistakes and broken relationships. You're looking at a man who God used to give encouragement and hope to the hopeless, through the recognition of the realness of his transformation. A man who Christ empowered to stand as a leader, in the-midst of violent psychopathic lions. When you look at Face or experience his gift, God is showing you yourself. He's showing you that He will take you out of your deepest darkness, deepest pain, deepest failure, deepest identity crisis, enter you spiritually, cover you with His grace, enlighten your mind, touch your tongue and hands, and teach them to be productive. He will touch your heart and teach you to love and to smile again. He will touch everyone around you and give you favor with them. When you experience Face, understand that his face is your face, and that it is seeking the face of God that allows us to become empowered to move and love beyond our perceived limitations. God is real.

Let your pain mold you... Let your pain become God's platform... Let your pain become the foundation Christ uses to build a bridge to reach others after you... *Analyze that*

"Blessed"

Blessed

"Blessed" just blessed me with 6 pages... The most profound, well-rounded, spiritually grounded piece I've read in ages... Prose of a poet, theology of a pastor, wisdom of the sages... Elocutionary excellence of orators on grand stages... Perspective of a reporter in-the-eye-of-the-storm as it rages... Authenticity of one who has obviously paid his dues but been denied his wages... I can imagine the look of surprise on the face of haters as their collective eyebrow raises... But I'm not here to sing his praises... Or undermine the truth that the sole recipient of all glory is Jesus... But to underline the evidence of the power of God conveyed through a willing vessel who decreases, as He increases... To remind my readers that to achieve this, we must die daily, for the struggle is ceaseless... *Our gifts are not our own...* But given that we may use them to glorify our King, who sits upon the throne... & *this is not our home...* This broken, dying world, where the Prince of Darkness roams... But we grow so comfortable here, w our nice homes and our iPhones... We drive cars and fly drones... With each advancement our pride has grown... As we strive toward our will and our masterplans... We stray from the Divine will of our Master's Plan... Yet, we audaciously call ourselves masterminds... Well you can seek to master yours, while I strive to allow Christ to master mine... Know ye not that ye are God's- apostrophe? Or have you traded Him like a commodity...? In favor of your ideologies & philosophies...? That deify and pay homage to self, with your idiosyncrasies and oddities? Probably...

Unfortunate if my artistry offends you, but I'm into apologetics, not apologies... The evidence is evident - His Eminence is imminent... Christ is King, no matter who is President ... & I don't hesitate to tell you He is Heaven-sent ... He touched me - and I been representing ever since...

2/26/16

Under the Microscope

"I'm here because my codefendant snitched on me." "My chick was mad because I cheated, so she lied on me." "My lawyer threw me under the bus."

I hear these excuses daily. I offered many of them up in explanation of my *own* plight for years. I still catch myself doing it from time to time, only to a lesser degree.

"We lost because he wasn't playing defense." "He wouldn't pass the ball." "I lost the chess game because there were too many people on the sideline distracting me."

Pride. Fear of diminished self-image. Saving face. We justify our failures and *undermine* when we *underperform* for a myriad of reasons. In doing so, we perpetuate our failures. We employ defense strategies in order to safeguard ourselves against the shame of future failure. We follow up *insufficient performances* with *inadequate excuses. But I've learned* something:

"People Want Results, Not Excuses"

Watch any major sporting event. Upon conclusion of any competitive match, reporters seek out the victor, or a member of the winning team... "What's your secret?" "How did you prepare for this team?" "When you released that game-winning shot, and you realized it was going in, what was going through your mind?"

"People Want Results, Not Excuses"

Yet, we waste incredible amounts of time justifying, excusing, and minimizing our failure. We damage relationships because we point fingers at teammates, coworkers, spouses... Our lawyer, our codefendant, our victim, our pastor, the police, the judicial system, the President... Some of us go as far as to blame God.

"Denial is not a *river* in *Egypt;* it is an *ocean* in *America,* where millions are drowning..."

I am 30 years old. And as a result of a truly miraculous sequence of events, spanning over the last 13 and ½ years of my life, I have a 2nd chance at life. *Failure is not option...* notice, I said *failure,* not *failing. Failing* is okay. *Failing* is inevitable. But failure is when failing becomes acceptable, normal, commonplace...

"Failure is Not an Option"

Excuse won't suffice. Blame-shifting won't cut it. If I am to be successful, 100% accountability for my failure is essential. Even my failed attempts must be viewed progressively- dissected, analyzed, and used to advance along the road to success.

But that requires a paradigm shift concerning failure. It requires switching the lens through which we view failure. It requires seeing failure not as an end, but as means to an end... It requires seeing failure not as a final destination, but as an inevitable pit-stop on the road to success...

I have 24 felonies. I am guilty of them all. I was not caught because my codefendant told on me - I was arrested because I committed crimes. I was not rail-roaded - I received far less time than I deserved. I am a decent chess player. When I win, it is because of a good move, a well-executed strategy, or capitalizing on an opponent's mistake... When

I lose, it is *my fault*. Or, I was simply bested by a superior strategist... Acknowledging that is the first step in improving my game.

It isn't easy to be objective about my losses or failures. I have a lot of pride. But my hunger for success trumps my pride. My family needs me. My loved ones are depending on me. Expectations are high. My support system is strong, and they believe in me.

These are incredibly powerful motivating factors. My motivation to succeed is exponentially greater than my fear of failure. There is far too much at stake for false pride.

"To Whom Much is Given, Much is Expected."

We owe it to our family. We owe it to our loved ones. We owe it to ourselves. Above all, we owe it to God - who has given us all that we have - to do all that we can, to be the best that we can. There are too many who are incapable of succeeding, to settle for failure and excuses for failure. We have to put our psychology involving excused failure under the microscope, to learn the underlying causes that hinder us from reaching our potential. Then, those inspired by our success can put it under the microscope & see the failure, resolve, resilience, dedication, repetition, hunger, struggle, pain, set-backs, comebacks & patience necessary to achieve success. *"Put it Under the Microscope"*

3/3/16

Please... Come!!

The B.L.O.O.D.S. and Z.M.F. (Zoe Mafia Family) are at war. Three weeks ago, a ZMF member stabbed a BLOOD 10 times. He lived. 2 weeks ago, a BLOOD stabbed a Z.M.F. member 17 times. He lived. Y.A.M.M. is the youth program on this prison compound that Face and I lead. Last weekend they were in the building *strapped* (carrying knives), drama kicked off, and a dude *clutched* (reached for his knife). I got in between them in time, but the police still saw the static. Last night we explained that this cannot happen again -Thursday nights at Y.A.M.M. has to be neutral grounds. They all agreed. All the gang leaders are in the room, 6 different gangs. The leader of the gang that started the scuffle begged me to allow him to address the group. He apologized. The face of humility is never shown by them in-the-midst of their enemies... Then, he said he wouldn't be the reason security shuts the program down. In the group discussions, one young gang member stated openly, in the presence of his enemies, "I want to be like you and Face - intelligent but gutter. Christlike, but fearless". It blew me away that he conceded his admiration for our walk in the presence of his enemies. Unheard of. These young cats have blood on their hands, bodies under their belts, ice on their hearts, bullet wounds on their skin. Another gang member said, "I'm tired of being a follower. I wanna lead like you and Face". That came from a young man known by the moniker "Chopper City", earned by his reputation for killing 3 of his enemies with an AK-47 at age 17.

For the first time in their life, they are seeing Christians whose eyes also reflect their journey through the soulless streets they traveled through. They want to escape Egypt. They are ready to eat the Passover Lamb. They are ready for the blood on their doorposts. There are 70 of them in the room. There are 10 mentors, but the 70 are all seeking attention from Face and myself. We only have 2 hours a week - and there are 70 of them. One tells me of his mother's death; he wants to talk. Another is struggling with addiction to spice; he wants to talk. One wants to leave his gang, but he's scared; he wants to talk. Another wants to know what books I've read; he wants to talk. One wants to know what my religious belief is; he wants to talk. Another just passed his G.E.D.; he wants to talk. One goes home in 30 days, needs some words of encouragement; he wants to talk. They all want talk... But we only have 2 hours. And there are 70 of them.

Where are you Christian soldiers?! If you're out there, *we need you in here!* The generation of youth they say are beyond hope? They're here, and they want to talk. Those who they say won't listen? They want to talk! Are you listening to me?! They are ready to listen to you. Yes, they have blood on their hands. But they respect the Blood of the Lamb, when His power is being lived out by "God's sons". We need more young Christians coming into the prisons. The harvest is plenty, but the laborers are few. I see them watching me every day from the opposite side of the chow hall. I see how they watch Face as he walks the compound. I see how they check out the authentic bond between Face and me when we vibe. They want to cross over. Right here, right now, we have a chance to allow Christ to impact an entire generation of youth, but we gotta get *out of* the churches and *into* the streets, detention centers and prisons. When these cats see Christ walked powerfully by their peers, it allows them to visualize living for Christ while still enjoying their youth - the exact opposite of what they believe submission to Christ to be. One young man who spoke up in the program last week, ran (ran) up to me the next day and said, "all my life I received accolades for being violent. After speaking last night, my friends have been expressing admiration for my positive message". Then he had me holding back tears when he said, "Man I feel good about myself! You encourage me by how you living, and Face got me wanting to try to write some poetry!" All we did was live out Christ, and give them an environment where a higher set of standards is demanded. Men of God, women of God: *We need you in here!* Come! Face didn't ask me to write this. He left the room, left the journal on the table, and these words left my heart, leaving these pages stained with ink, ink which is the representation of the blood of the youth who have been killed in a gang war, in a prison, because you felt Christ sending you here, but you would not come... Please... Come!

"Blessed"

The Awakening

It has begun... Like the stirring of the ashes, from which the Phoenix emerges, after its 5-year slumber... Not the spreading of the wings – not yet... just merely the stirring of the ashes... Not yet freedom, but the process from which freedom will result inevitably... They said I'd never be free again!! They assumed that my life had been consumed by the flames of my own self-destruction... And that all that remained were memories, which time and circumstance would eventually erase, like strong winds scattering the ashes of the phoenix... Twelve years, seven months, five days, and the ashes are stirring... They said it was over, and I believed them... I believed it was over... I thought life, as I knew it, had come to an end... And, in a sense, it did. Twelve years, 7 months, and 5 days of oppression... Of suppressing my desires. Desires to live, to love, and to laugh as I choose! To make my own decisions. To define myself. To come and go, when and where I choose... To express myself how I see fit, through my speech, my wardrobe, my style, my personality...

When the gavel slams & the sentence is imposed, life
as you know it ends... Parts of you must *die*. Certain
passions, preferences and tastes must die.

But *The Awakening* has begun... The passions and preferences
are coming to life... The ashes are stirring. Freedom is
imminent – I can taste it, I can feel it in every fiber of my
being! *I am alive!* I will go where I choose to go, when I choose

to go… I will wear what I want. I will speak my mind. I will feel the caress of a woman! I will spread my wings!!!

Not just yet… But the ashes are stirring. Freedom is within my grasp. Twelve years, seven months, five days… Under one year remaining…

The Ashes are Stirring…

Release Therapy

For the last 13 years and 4 months of my life, my thoughts have been unwaveringly fixated upon one thing... One desire, one pursuit, one motivation... One compelling force that has dictated every action, as a puppet master dictates the movements of the marionette... One wish, one dream, one fantasy, one obsession... It is the obsession of every man, of every woman - Black, White, Hispanic... Whether old, young, Christian, Muslim, Atheist- who has been fettered by the immense weight of incarceration... It is the common thread... It is the collective obsession, hunger, thirst, need!!! It is *"Freedom"!!!*

Not freedom as in some abstract, or complex, or philosophized definition . But freedom in its most basic, primitive, fundamental form... Freedom as in the absence of chains, shackles, & fences. Freedom as in the ability to move in any direction, at any moment one desires... Freedom as in the authority to make one's own decisions and manage one's own life, in even the most trivial arenas; what one wears or eats...

I have dreamt of freedom... Dreams so real that my awakening was akin to re-incarceration... As though the pain and trauma experienced, at the time of my arrest, occurred anew upon exiting a dream of freedom, into the reality of my captivity... I have petitioned the courts for my freedom. I have called upon the Almighty God with fervent prayer and supplication for my freedom. I have cried for my freedom. The lust for physical freedom is consuming. The heart's cry for freedom is deafening... The soul's yearning for freedom is maddening ... It seems one can think of nothing else. One desires nothing else... Freedom can become your taskmaster. Freedom can become your slave master... Freedom can become your God.

I have seen countless men die in chains while awaiting freedom. I have seen countless more lay old of it, only to squander it and spend the rest of their natural lives wallowing in regret and self-pity, futilely attempting to project blame onto someone other than themselves...I have watched precious few men face their plight boldly and courageously, determined to live purposefully and meaningfully, whether or not freedom comes... I have witnessed even fewer *obtain* it, *maintain* it, and make the most of it...

My Freedom is Upon Me

& I wonder, "what will my legacy be when the last entry is made in the last chapter, and the book of Face closes..." What will my testimony look like? Will I be another tragic example of what *not* to do? Will I become an inspiration for what is possible when a man - covered with the grace of Christ, indwelled with the Holy Spirit, purposed and endowed by God to overcome tremendous adversity and overwhelming odds - commits himself to break cycles, shatter statistics, break chains, and empower others?"

Certainly, I would desire the latter. But there is a difference between freedom the *fantasy* and freedom the *reality*... Freedom the *reality* brings incredible responsibility with it. One becomes so acquainted with the fantasy of freedom - so familiar with the dream of freedom -that the reality of it is a stranger or a foreigner... & one may not know what to do with it, when one lays hold of the very thing they've pined for ... We *hope* and *pray* for freedom, but most fail to adequately *prepare* for it.

My Freedom is Upon Me

I am nervous. I am afraid of failure. I am anxious. I am excited. I am experiencing a myriad- no! a kaleidoscope - of emotions. They bombard me in waves, in torrents. *And I embrace them all.* I allow each emotion to be absorbed into every fiber of my being. I allow the fear, the anxiety, the doubt, the uncertainty to wash over me and run freely. Because each are forces and sources of energy that I must convert into fuel, into motivation... "All Things Work Together for the Good of Those Who Love God..." Emboldened by that truth, I work to use all things for good - even the bad.

My Freedom is Upon Me

& it is not the rose-colored fairytale that I have often fantasized that it would be... There is no confetti, no parade, no red carpet... No cameras. I will emerge with no wings, no magic wand, no fortune... In fact, as I survey the landscape, the terrain I am set to re-enter... Its almost anticlimactic...

My family is struggling. My mother is sick, old, and poor. My brother is lost and struggling to find meaning in this world. My sister is depressed, disillusioned, and courageously trying to pick up the pieces, after another failed relationship and disappointment. My best friend - after 10 years of integrity, fidelity, determination, resilience and obedience to Christ - is *fallen.* Terribly, fearfully, dangerously, *fallen.*

And reality has set in. Life, whether in chains, or "free", is a struggle... People are hurting. My loved ones are broken and suffering. Life, no matter where it is lived on this Earth, is a constant struggle... Joy, pain, triumph, defeat, elation, despair, mountains, valleys, losses... But...

Life is a Beautiful Struggle

The struggle has made me strong. The struggle has made me wise. The struggle has cultivated within me patience, strength, resilience, resolve, and humility. The struggle has kept me grounded and made me solid. The struggle has caused me to pay attention to detail, to appreciate the little things, to keep getting up, to respect the struggle of others. The struggle has taught me to love, and not judge. The struggle has become my teacher, my coach, my companion... The struggle has equipped me. My Freedom is Upon Me... *I am ready.*

2/29/16

End of Sentence...

Less than 48 hours from now, I will be released from the Florida Department of Corrections, after serving 13 years, 8 months and 3 weeks, on a 15-year sentence... I was arrested at the age of 17, faced life plus over a hundred years, received 15 years at the age of 18, served my sentence at 9 different institutions with over 10,000 men... I entered in my teens and I will emerge in my 30s... My entire 20s were spent chained to the sidelines of life, watching the world continue unhindered by my absence... Loved ones growing old, loved ones growing up... Peers passing me by, peers passing away... I myself began this journey young, arrogant, lost, angry, defiant... Almost 14 years later, I emerge as a man of faith - tempered by the fiery trials, anchored by the storms... Strengthened from the results of heavy burdens, carry for great distances, over long periods of time... Humbled by, not only repeated exposure to the humiliation that accompanies being an inmate and a number, but also (most important) being made aware of my sins, crimes and brokenness in the presence of an Almighty God... Educated through study, wisened through experience ... Fortified through adversity. I have become intimately acquainted with loneliness, pain, disappointment, need and sorrow... Watching men go home, awaiting my time, watching men die, wondering if I would never make it out.... *And, now, my time has come.*

I'm counting down hours for the moment when I will have paid my debt to society with finality, when I leave this hostile environment, when the prison gates open and I walk into the next chapter of my life. My family and loved ones will await me outside the fences. I will be *free!!* Everyone - my family, my loved ones, my cellmates, my friends -want to know how I feel.... Everyone wants to know what's going through my mind, what it must feel like... Impossible to describe or articulate... But I will try...

I feel like laughing. I feel like crying. I feel like dancing. I feel like being still... Shouting, being silent.... I want to talk to everyone, and no one... I want to do everything & nothing. Paradoxical, yet true...

I feel like laughing at all of those who said I'd never make it, and who wanted me to fail. I feel like crying for all my brothers and friends I leave behind, who may never make it home. I feel like dancing in celebration of a future that is bright, promising, and limitless... I feel like being still and allowing the bigness of this moment - this opportunity- to be absorbed into my very marrow... I feel like shouting in triumph for having overcame... I feel like being silent, in awe of a Savior merciful enough to erase my guilt, wash away my shame, and avoid a second chance to someone as undeserving as me... Meditating on His amazing grace. I want to talk to all of my partners, bid them farewell, share a few last moments, create a few more memories... But my words would open wounds - a reminder that I am going home to pursue my dreams, while they continue in their nightmares.... So that any word I speak sounds like bragging, or patronizing, or at best, some hollow platitude.... So I want to be alone, to avoid those awkward exchanges that occur between friends, when one's situation suddenly and drastically improves, as the other's remains unbearable.... When one feels guilty over his good fortune, and the other becomes envious of it... And I don't want to feel guilty. I've been accused and found guilty for 14 years...

So, I prefer to talk to no one. I want to do anything and everything to keep me busy and keep my mind off the clock, which is moving excruciatingly, impossibly slow... But there is nothing left in prison to do, except leave... So, I'm suspended between 2 realities...

I feel like the phoenix, preparing his wings to fly out of the ashes of self-destruction and soar to new heights! I feel like the Count of Monte Cristo, emerging from the dark loneliness of my cell after 14 years -wisened, enlightened, strengthened, driven -to begin life anew! I feel like Lazarus, being called forth from my tomb and casting off my grave clothes, to dine in-the-midst of my loved ones, in the presence of my Savior. I feel blessed. I feel humbled. I feel anxious. I feel overwhelmed. I feel expectant. I feel victorious. I feel weary from the journey, yet ready for the race. I feel... I feel... I feel... Ugh!!! I don't even know what I feel...

8/25/16

Final Lap

For years, I was a poet on a shelf... An idle artist, who could have been painting portraits of self... So that even those who can't see my face can still read my *Face Expressions* ... A faithful messenger delivering sacred messages... Committing unto faithful men these faith-filled lessons... Leaving road signs along the way for guidance to those traveling in the same direction... That you may *grow* and *improve*... & choose to present your lives as living sacrifices to He who has chosen you... That the image of Christ could be made whole in you... Now, I'm attempting to impart what's been overdue... If this journal was an actual portrait of me... I pray I'm conformed enough into His image that my audience could see the Lord in me... That the Face Expressions captured in these pages' reflections... Portray and attest to spiritual features which resemble The Savior's essence... Son of Bonnie, seed of Elijah, but I wanna look like Jesus... Joshua - conqueror, disciple, leader... Who looks to Christ to lead him, and hungers for Christ to feed him... Willing to give my life, if need be... In fact, I'm anxious for Christ to greet me, arms wide to receive me... After He relieves me from this life here and frees me... There's a growing sense of urgency... I urgently urge you to concentrate on eternity... Like every day is an emergency... & every lost soul is a patient awaiting surgery... To be made whole by The Master Physician... I lay my life upon the altar in an act of submission... My journal has become my confessional... I'm a poet, but no professional... A spiritual man - not an intellectual, who overstates sentiments until they become ineffectual... My pen is aimed at your heart, not your mental... My scars are testimonies of the hardships I've been through...

You gotta learn to play the cards He gives you... I was one of them hard-knock kids who never had a real mother or father I could cling to... Needless to say, I came up harder than most kids do... In the streets, where from the womb, they've already condemned you... To die young, or have them folks bar, chain and fence you... Where Satan roams, seeking to devour, and you just try not to be a part of the menu... Tears upon tears, years upon years... In the struggle, facing and overcoming fears... Forged in the fire, between a hammer and an anvil...

Stripped of my childhood but somehow managed to be a man still... Discarded like refuse in a landfill... Landed in Never Never Land - I understand how Peter Pan feels... To whom much is given, much is expected... Hope springs eternal where love is injected... Charlie, Brenda, Manda Faye, Judah Leon...

Bonnie, Nicole, Asher, Brione... & everyone who held me down and helped me cope behind the wire... In memory of the soldiers who fell here, like Earl and Fyah... In dedication of those in chains, waiting to be free... Otto, Marty P, Big Lou, Zone 3... Mazer, Wine, Jeffery Jr., and "E... A tribute to you all for what you've contributed to me... Though this journal is concluded, the journey of faith progresses... They wait with abated breath on the next *Face Expressions*.

Free at Last!!

I made it! I've been home for over 4 ½ years now. It's been a long, tumultuous, uphill battle. But the rewards of enduring have proven to be exponentially greater than the struggles. I have had some amazing opportunities since my release, and have included some pictures just to attest to God's faithfulness. I began writing in a prison cell. I spent 15 years being viewed as nothing more than a number… But God is faithful, and He uses the foolish things of the world to confound the wise. He took me from prison to purpose. From an inmate, to a father. An artist. A poet. A mentor to at-risk youth. And we can officially add published author to the list. He is able! He will restore the years that the locusts have eaten. He will repair relationships that we have destroyed. He will reach waaay down – rock bottom of the very bottom of the pit… Down into the miry clay. And He will touch you. He will heal you. He will do exceedingly more than you could ever imagine. He can free you! And who The Son sets free, is free indeed!

The 3 pieces that follow weren't written in prison. They were written by me, for a few of the events I have been blessed enough to be a part of. The first is C.2.T.R., and was written and performed with The Voice's season 13 3rd place winner, Brooke Simpson, at Potential Church, Cooper City. The second is entitled "I Have a Dream for You", and was written for the youth at the Ft. Myers Dream Center. The 3rd was written for an annual pastor's conference on fatherhood/identity, and is entitled "W.Y.S.I.A."

C. 2. T. R.

Staring into the world through the window pane... I see the hidden pain on the faces in the picture frame... I see they're not in prison, but they're still in chains... Chained to the rhythm, praying for a rhythm change... Some stand for nothing, so they fall for anything... Seeking what they cannot see, because their vision's stained... And we could never Your frames but Jesus – could You please give us some bigger frames? He's the Doctor, He can make you see... He can stop the music, break the chains, and set you free... Give you a new name and a new rep... Fit you for some new frames, some new specs... Introduce you to beauty you haven't viewed yet... Put you in a whole new lane, give you new step... You don't have to groove to that same ol 2 step... I keep my glasses out, but never block His rays... In my glass house, naked and unashamed...

I Have a Dream for You!

Young men:
"Yes Sir!!!"
Are Y'all Here?:
"We All Here!!!"
Can Y'all Hear?:
"We All Hear!!!"
I have a Dream for You:

"Tell us Your Dream!!!!"

I See Soldiers & Visionaries! Scholars, as well-versed in the Bible as the dictionary... Men w the faith of Abraham, the boldness of Paul, who refuse to be silent/Men who, when facing your lions, & bears, & Goliaths/ your hearts are like David- courageous, defiant/ facing your giants w faith that the Lion of Zion's behind you!/ I see Leaders Not caught up in repping the gang or the set where you came from/ Repping your Savior, loving your neighbor till death and the grave come/ And even they hold no STING for you!!!!
Jesus seized those keys so He could let Freedom RING for you/ A feat not even the great Doctor King, but only the King of Kings could do/ Young men:
"Yes Sir!!!"
I have a Dream for You!!!

"Tell Us Your Dream!!!"

I See Game Changers!!! Contributing to the advancement of modern technology/ I see scholarships, I see you learning and teaching in colleges/ increasing in wisdom and knowledge like Solomon/ I see Lenders, not borrowers/Leaders, not followers/ In a world filled w wolves, I see sheep who're not swallowed up/ I see entrepreneurs, businessmen, some gifted w industry/ I see athletes, actors, authors, some called into ministry/

Young Ladies:
"Yes Sir!!!"
Are Y'all Here?:
"We All Here"
Can Y'all Hear?:
"We All Hear!"
I have a Dream for You!!!
"Tell us Your Dream!!!"

I see Princesses & Queens in you/ Eve was the Mother of all living things, and I see her genes in you/ I see Proverbs 31 women, beautiful and virtuous/ knowing their identity, walking in their purposes/ I see young Women so hidden BEHIND Christ and HIS CROSS/ a young man has to seek Him to FIND YOU, or GET LOST/ Confident and Secure, no need to feed into hype/ or post selfies in pursuit of social media likes/ & those that do have a following are leading em right/ So when your admirers ARE watching they're seeing your light/ I see Backbones, Nurturers, Caregivers, Caretakers/ Bread winners, Bread Bakers, Homeowners, Homemakers/

Young Ladies:
"Yes Sir!!!"
I Have a Dream For You:

"Tell Us Your Dream!!!"

I See Game Changers!!! Contributing to the advancement of modern technology/ I see scholarships, I see you learning and teaching in colleges/ increasing in wisdom and knowledge like Solomon/ I see Lenders, not borrowers/ Leaders, not followers/ In a world filled w wolves, I see sheep who're not swallowed up/ I see entrepreneurs, businesswomen some gifted w industry/ I see athletes, actresses, authors, some called into ministry/

DreamCenter:
"Yes Sir!!!"
I Have a Dream for You!

In my Dream, I see you all, Defying the odds against you, not defined by what you've been through/ Striving, Thriving, Rising to your potential!!!/
In my dream, I see the Blood of Jesus and the Spirit of the King in you/
I look at each of you, & I see He's placed a Dream in you!!!

DreamCenter:
"Yes Sir!!!!
    Tell Me Your Dream!!!

By Joshua T. Underwood

WYSIA

It's Christmas Eve of '89, I'm 4 yrs old, I'm happily unwrapping presents w my "family"/ Everyone is there, all laughing and caroling merrily/ Joy is in the air, but... In the midst of all the sharing, and everything that was happening/ I noticed the presence of a strange man who'd/ Entered our home, and was just standing there, empty-handed/ Quietly observing me as I'd nervously sneak glances/ I remember being unnerved by him staring at me/ Until he finally approached me, smiling sadly/

I glanced questioningly @ my father, who just looked back at me/ And said to me awkwardly but candidly..."Son... Say hello to your Daddy"... Those words rocked me, As you can imagine, in that moment I was confused/ My world turned upside down, I was lost, my soul felt bruised/ And because I didn't know what else to do/ I Looked at who I THOUGHT was my father like, "But Wait a minute!!! You told me that YOU!!!!/ Were MY "DADDY"!!! You even made me rehearse it over and over w YOU!!!/ But now you're saying HE is my father, and I don't even KNOW THIS DUDE!!!

Needless to say, from my earliest memories/ Among many things, I wrestled w my identity/ I struggled w even having the ability to definitively/ Define what the word "Father" meant to me/ Because even tho my "REAL" father was a rolling stone, known to roam here, there, and EVERYWHERE/ Me & Mama were always out and about, bouncing from house to house, but somehow HE was still NEVER

THERE/ I slept on countless floors and couches, wearing dirty hand-me-downs, w lice-infested hair/ in crime-infested hoods, drug infested homes, inhaling smoke-infested air/ & tho my "foster father" would, arbitrarily pull us outta the fire, far too often, he left us THERE!/ So at the age of 17... I found myself crumbling under the weight of the cross I'd been left to bear.../ See, although childhood I.Q. tests resulted in me being labeled what they call "gifted"/ My mother was addicted... And I was just this/ Poor little snotty nosed misfit mixed kid/ Early on, I wasn't so much a "Problem Child" as I was a child w problems/ Exposed to trauma, coping w internal conflicts, and my I.Q. couldn't solve em/ So as I grew, my issues began evolving/ & eventually, started to manifest themselves in the lifestyle I got involved in/I was drifting, broken, blind, w no vision/ at the time, I grabbed almost any kind of drug I could find, & I did it/ to numb the pain, or my conscience towards the sins & crimes I committed/ I admit it, I crossed lines, & created victims/ I'd commit the crime, & try to escape the sentence/ until my last time trying to escape ended.../ w an officer performing in the line of duty injured/ & me in solitary confinement, facing the rest of my life in prison/ alone in my cell, stripped of my foolish pride/ everyone including the evening news at 5/ are speaking over my life, I don't know what's truth or lies, or where the 2 Collide/ But I do know... I am desperate- it's literally "Do or Die/ I'm 17, planning my final escape- Contemplating Suicide/

I am broken
Somehow still breaking
I barely have strength left to stand

And these voices
Say I won't make it
Playing in my head like a band

I am hopeless
I am shaking
W the Instrument of death in my hand

But You spoke to me
& You saved me
I was drowning, You gave me your hand!!!

Jesus, You told me
"Son, be patient
This is all a part of My plan

Though you're like Jonah
Overtaken
I'll again place your feet on dry land
Your life isn't Over!!!
Just wait & see!
Truth is, your life just began!!

My Son, I've chosen you
So that they can see
I can do in you what no one else can"

And all other voices
Began Fading
At the Word of the Great I Am

He took a broken me
began shaping me
My life became clay in His hands

He placed a hope in me
He put faith in me
& over time, turned the boy into a man

Lord, You know me!!
You prepare a place for me
You engrafted me into Your family

Abba, You are Holy
You're My Savior
My Father, The Lion & Lamb!!!!

I am Chosen
Not Forsaken
Lord, I am who You say I am!!!!

Joshua Underwood
Pastor's Conf. '18
NLC DreamCenter

Printed in the United States
by Baker & Taylor Publisher Services